"In our world so fraught with division and despair, Jordan Denari Duffner's experiences bring a fresh insight into Muslim-Catholic relations. In addition to recounting her many positive encounters with people of the Muslim faith, Jordan shares her insights in the ways that her own Catholic faith has deepened as a result. This book is an oasis of hope and a must read by all who take seriously the need for dialogue and understanding, particularly between Muslims and Catholics."

— Bishop Mitchell T. Rozanski, Emeritus Chair of the Bishops' Committee on Ecumenical and Interreligious Affairs

"In a time of political division and fear, Jordan Denari Duffner offers us a refreshing work of love, compassion, and understanding. *Finding Jesus among Muslims* is an open invitation for all of us to better un͟ r shared values and the powerful beliefs that unit͟ an help all of us become peacemakers, lov͟ and heal what has been torn apart."

— Martin O'Malley, Former gov͟ presidential candidate

"*Finding Jesus among Muslims* is ͟ully written and honest testimony to the value and power of interreligious learning, grounded in Jordan Denari Duffner's own life experience, reflection, and prayer. It recounts in lucid terms the place of Islam, its piety, and friendship with Muslims in her journey as a young Catholic woman in the 21st century. That loving Islam has helped Duffner become a better Catholic will encourage many who find themselves today on the path between religions, encountering the new, yet finding their way home again. This fine addition to our growing library on interreligious learning is written with teaching in mind, and will be ideal for classroom use as well."

— Professor Francis X. Clooney, SJ, Parkman Professor of Divinity, Harvard University

"Jordan Denari Duffner's magnificent new book is a game-changer. Unlike so many 'interfaith' volumes where we are either talking at one another or attempting to demonstrate the superiority of our own tradition, this is a committed journey *with* one another. Duffner is passionately committed to not only learning *about* Islam and Muslims, but also *with* Islam and Muslims. A book like this could only be written by a committed Christian who shared a deep love for Muslims, and has genuinely, spiritually, and intellectually engaged both her own tradition and Islam. We do more than merely learn about religious traditions, we grow in faith as a result of journeying with Duffner. It is a moving, heartfelt, intellectually honest, and urgently relevant volume that moves us well beyond the usual parameters of the professional interfaith industry. Passionately and enthusiastically recommended for all Christians, Muslims, and people of faith who wish to live in a diverse world not in spite of our faiths, but because of them."

— Professor Omid Safi
Director, Duke Islamic Studies Center

Finding Jesus among Muslims

*How Loving Islam Makes Me
a Better Catholic*

Jordan Denari Duffner

LITURGICAL PRESS
Collegeville, Minnesota

www.litpress.org

26127

Nihil Obstat: Reverend Robert Harren, J.C.L., *Censor deputatis.*

Imprimatur: ✣ Most Reverend Donald J. Kettler, J.C.L., Bishop of Saint Cloud, October 27, 2017.

Cover design by Amy Marc.

1   2   3   4   5   6   7   8   9

Library of Congress Cataloging-in-Publication Data

Names: Duffner, Jordan Denari, author.
Title: Finding Jesus among Muslims : how loving Islam makes me a better Catholic / Jordan Denari Duffner.
Description: Collegeville, Minnesota : Liturgical Press, 2017. | Includes bibliographical references.
Identifiers: LCCN 2017041643 (print) | LCCN 2017020307 (ebook) | ISBN 9780814645932 (ebook) | ISBN 9780814645925
Subjects: LCSH: Missions to Muslims. | Christianity and other religions—Islam. | Islam—Relations—Christianity. | Catholic Church—Doctrines. | Islam—Doctrines.
Classification: LCC BV2625 (print) | LCC BV2625 .D84 2017 (ebook) | DDC 261.2/7—dc23
LC record available at https://lccn.loc.gov/2017041643

بسم الله الرحمن الرحيم

In the name of God,
the Most Compassionate,
the Most Merciful

Ad Majorem Dei Gloriam

For the Greater Glory of God

For my mother, who told me I had to write,
and for my father, who taught me how

Contents

Acknowledgments

I would like to thank the many people who have made this book possible. My husband, Chris, has been my spiritual companion since we met five years ago, and has been an unwavering supporter of my vocation. I'm grateful for our conversations that informed this book, and for his keen editorial eye.

My parents have encouraged my travels, interfaith exploration, and desire to be a writer since I was young. Over the years, they have read countless papers and articles, as well as drafts of the coming pages, providing critical feedback that improved my craft. My brother, too, has been a constant source of encouragement.

I am also grateful for the spirituality of the Jesuits and the Carmelites, and the members of these Catholic religious orders who have accompanied me in Indianapolis, Indiana, Washington, DC, and Amman, Jordan. I also owe much to the numerous Catholic priests and laypeople, both living and deceased, who have given me an example of how to live as a committed Catholic in communion with Muslims.

I am immensely thankful to all those who have read drafts of this book, given suggestions and pointers, sat down for interviews, and shared openly with me about their relationship with God. I give sincere thanks to Barry Hudock and Liturgical Press for approaching me to write this book. Their offer to work with them confirmed a vocation I have long felt called to.

And, of course, I am perpetually grateful for the companionship of my many Muslim friends, who continue to reveal to me truths about God that transcend—yet are deeply manifested in—our different religious traditions. Thank you for inviting me to encounter God with you.

Notes on Translation and Terms

Throughout this book, I often use Arabic words that may be unfamiliar to Christian readers. These terms—many of which come from Muslims' scripture, the Qur'an—are important to learn for understanding the religion of Islam. I always define these terms upon first use, and put them in italics. To aid readers with this new terminology, I have included a glossary in the back of the book. Additionally, since some readers might be unfamiliar with the names of Muslim friends I mention, I have also included a list of given names with their pronunciation and meanings at the end of the book. The book's index can also aid readers in locating references to significant topics.

Here, I should define some of our basic terms: *Muslim* and *Islam*. To put it most simply, a *Muslim* is someone who adheres to the religion of *Islam*. But these words have deeper meaning in the Arabic language from which they come. (Arabic is a Middle Eastern language related to Hebrew, the language of much of the Bible, and Aramaic, the language Jesus spoke.) In these "Semitic" languages, concepts are contained in three-letter roots that are used in different formulations to form words with related meanings. Both "Muslim" and "Islam" come from the root *s-l-m*, which means peace. This is not only a peace that connotes physical security or the absence of war, but also an interior, spiritual state of calm, trust, reassurance, wholeness, and harmony. *Islam* is the act of giving one's self over to God, and aligning one's own will with God's; a *Muslim* is a person who willfully undertakes this act of devotion, and experiences the peace that comes with it. (In the Qur'an, Jesus and his disciples are counted as "Muslims.") The idea at the root of these Arabic words is why many

Muslims describe Islam as a "religion of peace." The word "Islamic" is an adjective used in English to describe inanimate things related to the religion of Islam, like history, art, or a community center.

For some Arabic words and Islamic concepts I discuss in the book, I use the English translation. When referring to God, for example, I don't use *Allah*, which simply means "God" in Arabic, but rather use the English word that readers are familiar with. I have made this choice to mitigate the confusion and sense of difference that often arises when words in foreign languages are used to describe otherwise familiar concepts.

Because the book is directed primarily at a Catholic and Christian audience, when I use the word "we," it usually refers to people who identify as Christian. I have made this choice reluctantly, since I am aware of the tendency for my faith community to treat Muslims as an outside group. This decision is not meant to reinforce an "us-versus-them" dichotomy, but rather to enable me to speak clearly to my own Christian community.

Kenneth Cragg's *Readings in the Qur'ān* served as the basis for the translations of Qur'anic passages in this book. In some cases, Cragg's translations were adjusted for clarity. *The Study Quran*, edited by Seyyed Hossein Nasr, and English translations compiled on Quran.com were also consulted in rendering the Qur'an into English for this book.

In the Qur'an, God refers to himself using three different pronouns: the third-person "He," the first-person "I," and the first-person "We." The use of "We" should not be understood as referring to multiple gods; rather, it connotes God's honor and greatness. (Comparably, use of the royal "We" was common among royalty in Europe.) As in Judaism and Christianity, God in Islam is understood to be singular, one. Though the use of "We" might be surprising for those encountering the Qur'an for the first time, readers should see God using "We" in the Qur'an as no different from using "I."

Throughout the book, I use transliteration—the process of rendering the letters of one alphabet into another—when writing Arabic words in English. I have attempted to use spellings that best mimic the pronunciation in Arabic. Alternative spellings and further details on pronunciation are included in the glossary or list of names when necessary. Transliterations of *al*, the Arabic word for "the," for example, will sometimes appear *ar* or *as*, depending on the word that follows it. This is due to an Arabic linguistic convention that allows for ease of pronunciation. Thus, the phrase "the Entirely Merciful," one of the attributes Muslims use to refer to God, is transliterated *ar-Rahman*, with *r* rather than with *l*.

Like Hebrew, the Arabic language does not have capital and lowercase letters. Still, as is common practice among Muslims writing in English, I capitalize proper nouns relating to the divine or to honored figures like the Prophet Muhammad.

Readers will notice that there are different spellings of the name Muhammad throughout the text. For the Prophet Muhammad, the spelling "Muhammad" is used. For other people mentioned in the book who share the Prophet's name, I spell it the way they do (e.g., Mohamed, Mohammad, etc.).

Readers will also notice the usage of *dh* in the transliterated word for the Islamic call to prayer, or *adhan*. The *dh* sound resembles the "th" sound in the words "the" or "than," not "three."

Readers will also notice my use of the words "interfaith" and "interreligious" throughout the book. Though some theologians have unique definitions for these terms, I will use these two words interchangeably. Interfaith, which is often used in American contexts to describe relationships between people of diverse religious backgrounds, is a word readers might be more familiar with. Interreligious is the term the Catholic Church uses to talk about its interactions with other religions.

Introduction

Interfaith Dialogue
Walking Together Toward Truth

All Christian communities are called to practice dialogue.
—Pope St. John Paul II, *Redemptoris Missio* (57)

On the edge of a vast salt lake on the Mediterranean island of Cyprus sits a small mosque. Nestled in a grove of palm trees, it is dedicated to a seventh-century woman named Umm Haram. She was an aunt of the Prophet Muhammad, who Muslims believe was a messenger of God's revelation. During a trip to Cyprus in 2016, I walked into the courtyard, where the mosque was surrounded by brightly painted yellow buildings with green trim. I took off my shoes in the shade of the domed roof and, though no one asked me to, I covered my head with the scarf I had brought with me and stepped sock-footed into the old mosque. Though the site is mainly visited by tourists now, its historical holiness was still palpable. This house of worship is believed to be the burial place of Umm Haram, and is considered to be one of the holiest sites for Muslims, after the mosques in the cities of Mecca, Medina, and Jerusalem. Umm Haram, whose name means "honorable mother," had a close relationship with her nephew, Muhammad, and she is remembered as a generous and self-sacrificing person who served the poor.[1]

As I walked into the mosque and across the patterned carpet, I noticed the *mihrab*, the curved alcove cut into the wall that is a central feature of all mosques. Resembling the niche, or apse, in churches, the *mihrab* indicates the direction of Islamic prayer and points to the cube-shaped *ka'aba* in Mecca, thousands of miles away in the Arabian peninsula. The *ka'aba* marks the place that Muslims believe is the most sacred; it is the "house of God" on earth. According to Islamic tradition, the structure was originally built by the first man, Adam, then repaired by Abraham, and restored by Muhammad—all of whom are considered prophets. Every year, Muslims from around the world converge on the *ka'aba* in a ritual of pilgrimage, to pray and to cultivate trust and dependence on God. Each Muslim person endeavors to make this pilgrimage, or *hajj*, at least once during one's life.

As I approached the *mihrab*, the focal point of the mosque, I felt an inclination to genuflect. I dropped down onto my right knee and made the sign of the cross, touching my fingers to my forehead, chest, and each shoulder. The feeling I had, standing before the *mihrab* in the Umm Haram mosque, is the same one I have felt hundreds of times in Catholic churches. Since childhood, I have experienced a sense of reverence when approaching the consecrated Host, the Body of Christ, stored in the gilded tabernacle. A similar feeling also wells up in me today when I enter a mosque, like the one I visited in Cyprus, or when I hear the *adhan*, the melodic call to worship recited in Arabic before Islamic prayer. As I become aware of God's presence in that place or in that moment, I feel viscerally the need to bless myself with the sign of the cross to acknowledge it.

This recurring experience—of recognizing the divine in a setting defined by Islam, and responding with a gesture that is distinctly Catholic—grows out of countless encounters I've had with Muslims and their religion in recent years, both in the United States and in the Middle East. At Georgetown University, where I went to college, I made friends with students who were Muslim, and lived for a year in a dorm community for Muslim students. My roommate and I had long conversations about religion, but more often I connected with my Muslim friends over more familiar college traditions like playing basketball at the campus gym, attempting to make pancakes on the dorm stove, or procrastinating on homework by watching YouTube videos of cute animals.

During those years, as I studied theology, international affairs, and Arabic, I attended Islamic liturgies on occasional Fridays and festive dinners during the Islamic holy month of Ramadan. I also went on a retreat for Muslim students, and served on the Muslim Students Association board. Moved by the experiences I had dialoguing with peers and chaplains-in-residence who were Muslim, I became involved in the interfaith group on campus, in the hopes of facilitating for other students the kinds of encounters I'd been fortunate to have.

I also lived in the Middle Eastern country of Jordan, first as an undergraduate living with a host family for a semester, and again after college as a Fulbright researcher exploring Muslim-Christian relationships for a year. I talked about religion over tea with Jordanian friends I made in Amman, where I experienced a society shaped by Islam and where I also felt comfortable and supported in living out my Christian faith.

In the United States, I have interned and worked for organizations dedicated to improving understanding between Muslims and Christians, including the US Conference of Catholic Bishops. Particularly at the Bridge Initiative, where I worked for three years as a research fellow writing about anti-Muslim prejudice, Muslim colleagues became close friends and confidants with whom I could have deep discussions about God. Now, as a doctoral student studying Islam and Christianity, I continue these conversations with classmates and professors.

These experiences of interfaith dialogue—both formal and informal—have allowed me to grow in friendship with Muslims, and offered me a new approach to encountering God. And, in a way I didn't initially anticipate, these experiences have helped deepen my connection to my own Christian faith, too. My relationships with Muslims, my exposure to their faith, and my resulting reconnection to my Catholic roots draw me closer to God. This threefold blessing of interfaith dialogue is what this book is about.

Dialogue: A Fundamental Aspect of Being Christian

The Catholic Church teaches that interreligious dialogue is part of our vocation as Christians. Pope St. John Paul II insisted that dialogue is "fundamental" to the church's mission, a duty from which no person or parish is exempt.[2]

Why are we called to interfaith dialogue? And, why is it a part of our Christian vocation? We are called to dialogue because God dialogues. As Christians, we believe in one God who is also Trinity: Father, Son, and Holy Spirit. Saint Augustine understood this three-in-one God as a communication—or dialogue—of love, in which the Father and Son give and receive love, and the Holy Spirit is the love between them. God also dialogues with humanity. Throughout human history, God has revealed his love to us in countless ways. The Bible recounts beautiful stories of God dialoguing with figures like Abraham and Moses. Because we are made in God's image, and because we have received his love, we are called to imitate God's way of dialogue in our interactions with our fellow humans.

What is the end goal of this interfaith dialogue that all Christians are called to? Often, the reasons cited for engaging in dialogue are things like ending conflict, working for justice, collaborating to preserve religious freedom, improving mutual understanding of differences, or arriving at more definitive statements about common points of belief. All of these are important and beneficial outcomes of dialogue, but they should not be its impetus or its ultimate goal. Instead, dialogue should be driven by the desire to seek God together.

The goal of dialogue, like the rest of our life, is to grow closer to God. In interreligious dialogue, we undertake this journey toward God with Muslims or people of other faiths. Archbishop Michael Fitzgerald, the former head of the Vatican's interfaith council and a former Vatican ambassador to Egypt, writes that dialogue allows us to "help one another to respond to God's call."[3] As the Catholic Church teaches, to dialogue is "to walk together towards truth."[4]

The late Fr. Christian de Chergé describes Muslim-Christian dialogue as digging a well to the same source. Father de Chergé was a French Catholic priest, monk, and scholar who lived in a Cistercian monastery in rural Algeria in the 1990s. In 1996, he and his brother monks were killed during the country's civil war, after being captured by a rebel group. Before his death, he worked and prayed alongside his Muslim friends in the town. Father de Chergé borrowed the image of digging a well to God from his friend, Mohammed, who would often drop by the monastery and say, "It's been a long time since we've dug our well!"[5] Once, Fr. de Chergé asked Mohammed whether they would find Christian water or Muslim water at the bottom of the well. Mohammed answered that the water didn't belong to either faith group; rather, he said, the water they would find together is *God's*. For Fr. de Chergé, interreligious dialogue is born of the recognition that "the same thirst"—God—"draws us to the same well."[6] Believing that the ultimate destination of both Christians and Muslims is God, Fr. de Chergé also described dialogue as climbing on a ladder to God. One side-beam is Christianity, the other is Islam, and the many rungs are shared by both the Muslims and Christians who climb it.

What does this interfaith dialogue look like in everyday life? How are we—busy people who already do our best to serve our local community—supposed to engage in interfaith dialogue on top of everything else? For the Catholic Church, dialogue is not as much an activity as it is an attitude. More than an event to put on the schedule, dialogue is the open, friendly spirit that we bring to an encounter with someone of another faith. We might not realize it, but we participate in interreligious dialogue anytime we approach those of another faith with hospitality and love, ready to hear what others have to say. This can happen over meals, at the dentist office, in a school hallway, or in the grocery store.

When these kinds of neighborly encounters with people of other faiths occur in our ordinary, day-to-day activities, we are participating in what the church calls the "dialogue of life," which is considered the most important and the most common of four forms of dialogue that the church identifies in its teaching.[7] In addition to the dialogue of life, the church also encourages other, more formal ways of being in interfaith dialogue.

One of these forms is the dialogue of religious experience. It is about sharing experiences of prayer, worship, and other religious practices. It could involve attending Muslims' Friday liturgy, inviting Muslims to come to church, sharing about one's spiritual life, or even praying to God together. Reflecting together over passages of scripture from the Bible and the Qur'an and telling stories of inspiring saints or religious figures are other ways of sharing religious experiences.

This form of dialogue allows us to discuss what our relationship with God is like, and to get a window into how others relate to God.

Another form of dialogue is that of deeds and action. Motivated by our commitment to work for peace and justice in our communities, this form of dialogue entails working with people of other faiths to improve society and help all people flourish. Both Islam and Christianity have deep traditions of striving for social justice. When individuals of different religions collaborate to do community service, or when houses of worship team up to do good in their city, this is considered a form of interfaith dialogue.

The final form of dialogue centers around theological exchange. Usually described as a task for religious scholars or clergy, this type of dialogue is about more deeply understanding another's religious tradition and spiritual values. At their best, these formal conversations should not be preoccupied with arriving at hard-and-fast answers. Rather they should be approached as an opportunity for participants to listen intently to the other's point of view, articulate one's own beliefs, and see both religious traditions in a new way. Theological exchange should not just be reserved for experts; nonexperts should feel empowered to participate as well.

These four types of dialogue—the dialogue of life, of religious experience, of action, and of theological exchange—are encouraged by the Catholic Church in its teaching documents on interreligious encounters. In practice, these forms often overlap and should often be carried out together.

When we participate in dialogue, we do not intend to convert those of other faiths to Christianity. Father Tom Ryan, a veteran scholar of interfaith relations, explains that "dialogue does not seek the conversion of others to Christianity but the convergence of both dialogue partners to a deeper shared conversion to God."[8] In this sense, conversion is not changing one's religious community or affiliation but rather "the humble and penitent return of the heart to God in the desire to submit one's life more generously to Him."[9] To convert is literally to "turn around" or "turn toward." Dialogue allows all those involved to turn toward God together, and to deepen one's own religious commitment.

While the Catholic Church also encourages "proclamation," this task of sharing Christianity with others in the hope that they will become baptized Christians is a separate activity from dialogue. Dialogue is not done with ulterior motives and is not an instrument of proclamation. Dialogue and proclamation are two distinct activities of the church's broader mission.

It is worth reemphasizing that interfaith dialogue is not about converting others to Christianity, proving that we as Christians have all the answers, nor collaborating only for the sake of peace-building. At the core, dialogue is about growing closer to God. What we study in school, the career we choose, whether or not we choose to marry, and how we support our family are all ideally guided by this mission of deepening our relationship with God. The same is true of interfaith dialogue. Like everything else, dialogue should be rooted in and directed toward God, who John Paul II calls the "transcendent goal" that we have in common with people of other faiths.[10]

Interreligious dialogue allows us to grow closer to God in three ways: through the people we meet, through their religion, and through our own Christian faith. In dialogue, we learn to recognize God's Holy Spirit operating in those of other faiths, who are made in God's image. In dialogue, we are also given the possibility to encounter God through a faith tradition not our own. Finally, dialogue provides us an opportunity to reconnect with our Christian faith tradition. Questions and conversations that arise in dialogue may ignite our curiosity and spark a desire to delve more deeply into our own Catholic teachings and spirituality. Our friendships with those of other faiths and engagement with their religions can enrich our lives as Christians, and may even mean that we live out our Christianity in new ways that reflect the relationships we've built.

The Need to Dialogue with Muslims

This book focuses not on interreligious dialogue in a general way, but on dialogue with Muslims specifically. This is for a few reasons. First, this book centers on Islam because the Catholic Church—especially Pope Francis—has encouraged Christians to put special emphasis on dialogue with Muslims. In his first days as pontiff,

Francis expressed that it is "important to intensify dialogue [with Muslims particularly]" because "it is not possible to establish true links with God, while ignoring other people."[11] As the pope pointed out in his apostolic exhortation The Joy of the Gospel, there are more Muslims today living in historically Christian-majority societies than there used to be. Yet, in the United States at least, the vast majority of Catholics say they don't know any Muslims personally.[12] If we want to truly know God, the pope says, we must know our Muslim neighbors.

Second, the Catholic Church believes dialogue with Muslims should be a priority because of our shared religious beliefs and heritage. Christians and Muslims, along with Jews, believe in the one God, and we trace our religious roots to the figure of Abraham. (More similarities between Christianity and Islam will be laid out in chapter 1.)

Third, we as Christians have a special obligation to get to know those who are often misunderstood or feared. In my work researching anti-Muslim prejudice, I've observed that many Catholics, like other Americans, have lukewarm, if not negative, feelings toward Muslims, and most know very little about their religion. Many are also unaware of the impact that anti-Muslim prejudice has on the lives of ordinary Muslims. Dialogue offers us an opportunity to get to know and stand with people who we might perceive as the "other," beginning to view them as part of "us."

Lastly, this book focuses on Islam because dialogue with Muslims has been my own personal experience. Though I have been fortunate to know people who practice many different religions, the lessons I've learned about dialogue have occurred through my relationships with Muslims, both in the United States and in the Middle East. Islam has been the faith tradition that has most shaped my own experience.

While Muslim-Christian dialogue is the primary concern of this book, readers should recognize that the lessons of the book translate into interfaith dialogue with members of other religions, too. Immersion into another religious tradition, like Judaism or Sikhism, for example, can result in the same deepened relationship with God that I found among Muslims.

Drawn to God through Dialogue

As I have mentioned, Muslim-Christian dialogue can draw us to God in three ways: through our personal relationships with Muslims, who, like us, are created by God; through our encounter with the religion of Islam; and through our deepened connection to our Catholic Christian faith. This book is organized around these three blessings of dialogue, each addressed in two chapters.

Chapters 1 and 2 focus on our relationships with Muslims, who are made in God's image. To paraphrase Pope Francis, we Christians cannot truly be in relationship with God while being out of relationship with Muslims. Growing in friendship with Muslims means that we are willing to learn about the other, to allow each person to teach us something and reveal to us God's action in the world. In chapter 1, we begin this process of relationship-building by learning about Muslims' lives, particularly about their faith. I introduce readers to Muslims I have known, and present Islam as it has been presented to me—through the lived experiences of diverse individuals. I highlight aspects of Muslims' faith that are often overlooked, and draw particular attention to Islam's similarities with Christianity.

In chapter 2, we continue to get to know Muslims, including the prejudice that many in Western countries experience because of their religious affiliation or the way they look. Today, American Muslims living in the United States face discrimination that bears striking resemblance to the way Catholics were once treated in the US. In this chapter, I emphasize the importance of learning about Muslims' experiences of Islamophobia and also of acknowledging the way our stereotypes contribute to the suspicion and hostility that Muslims often face. We must be open to having our prejudices about Muslims challenged and our misconceptions dismantled. As Pope Francis reminds us in The Joy of the Gospel, our respect for Muslims "should lead us to avoid hateful generalisations" and to embrace them, especially refugees, with affection.[13] Growing in relationship with Muslims—learning about their joys and sorrows—reveals God to us. In dialogue, we encounter God with and through Muslims we meet.

We also encounter God through Muslims' religion, Islam. In chapters 3 and 4, I discuss how we can come to know God better through Islam, a religious tradition that is not our own. The Catholic Church acknowledges that God does not simply work in people, but also in their religions. When we participate in interreligious dialogue, we are witnesses to the reality of God working through other religions, teaching us something. In chapter 3, I talk about the ways my relationship with God has been deepened by my exposure to Islam. This has also been the experience of other Christians, even Catholic priests, and I share their stories. In chapter 4, I take a close look at some of the challenging theological topics that arise in Muslim-Christian dialogue, like the question, Do we believe in the same God? I also delve into differences in our creeds, and demonstrate that there are more similarities between our views of God than we are often led to believe.

The third section of the book—chapters 5 and 6—is about how dialogue helps us embrace and live out our own Christian faith in new and deeper ways. In chapter 5, I discuss how dialogue with Muslims propelled me to connect more deeply with God through my own tradition. Rather than pulling me away from Christianity, interreligious dialogue helped me approach my own religion with a fresh perspective and eager curiosity. Chapter 6 focuses on the rewards, challenges, and responsibilities of living as a Christian in dialogue with Muslims, how we might live our Christianity differently as a result of dialogue. At the end of the book, I also provide ideas and examples for putting interreligious dialogue into practice in one's own life, so that readers can carry the book's lessons into their daily activities. In the appendix, I also give questions that can be used to prompt personal reflection or group discussion. Additionally, I have provided a list of suggested readings and a prayer that can be used by Christians and Muslims in joint prayer.

I've chosen the title *Finding Jesus among Muslims* because it gets at the book's multilayered message and the reality of my own life: that dialogue with Muslims offers us the opportunity to deepen our relationship with God. Thanks to interreligious dialogue, I have found God—Jesus—in people who are Muslim, in their religion, and in the religion I grew up with: Catholicism.

This book is intended to be a facilitator of dialogue, to be a step along readers' journeys of faith. It can be read by individuals alone, or as a part of a course, book club, or prayer group. My hope is that it can speak to a broad audience, not just to Catholics or other Christians, though those groups are the book's primary audience. After reading the book, I hope my fellow Christians will feel empowered to reach out to Muslims in their local communities. I hope they gain new exposure to the Catholic Church's rich perspectives on dialogue, and find their relationship with God stretched and deepened. Non-Christian readers should also find the book encouraging, as it is rooted in my conviction that interreligious dialogue, no matter who is involved, can be an opportunity for discovering God in new ways. I hope Muslim readers in particular will feel affirmed by the book's message and by my deep appreciation for them and their faith.

Part I

MEETING GOD IN MUSLIMS

1

Mary, Mercy, and Basketball

Truly, [God] has chosen you [Mary]
above all women everywhere.

—Qur'an 3:42

In a small town in the north of Jordan, atop a hill surrounded by pine forests and olive groves, there is a shrine dedicated to the Virgin Mary. Known in Arabic as *Sayyidat al-Jabal*, or Our Lady of the Mount, the site overlooks the expansive Jordan River Valley and marks the place where Jesus, his mother, and his disciples are thought to have stayed during a journey from Jerusalem to the region of Galilee. For decades, Arab Christians have traveled on pilgrimage to the shrine to pray before the statue of the Blessed Mother, which many believe has been the source of miracles.

When I lived in Jordan, I visited the statue on pilgrimage with a few Filipina friends, who have worked for forty years in the Catholic Church's libraries in Jordan and Israel-Palestine. Under a sky blanketed by heavy clouds, we climbed the rolling hills of northern Jordan in a small car, and reached the Our Lady of the Mount compound, which also houses a school, church, and large room for veneration of the statue. There before the shrine, we prayed part of the rosary, surrounded by Orthodox-style icon murals depicting Jesus and Mary.

Our Lady of the Mount is not just a holy site for Christians. It is also a place of pilgrimage for Muslims. For those who practice Islam, Mary is an important religious figure whose name and story appear frequently in the Qur'an. Muslims revere her as the virgin mother of Jesus, and their holy text tells the story of the annunciation with striking similarities to the version in the Gospel of Luke. In the Qur'an, Mary asks the angel Gabriel, "How shall I bear a son when no man has known me?" (Qur'an 3:47).

Muslims see Mary as a model of faith. Like Catholics, they look to her as an example of someone who deeply trusted in God amid uncertainty and struggle. In the Qur'an, as in the Bible, Mary bears Jesus out of wedlock, facing scorn from her community. Maryam, as she's known in Arabic, is also honored for her intellect and deep spiritual connection to God. Chosen by God "above all women everywhere," the Qur'an says (4:32), Mary spent much time in solitude, praying in a place reserved especially for her in the sanctuary. The *mihrab*, the arched alcove in the mosque, is often associated with Mary's special place of prayer. In every Turkish mosque, there is a quotation from the Qur'an about Mary mounted above the arch. Because of Mary's centrality to the faith, many Muslim women and girls share her name, Maryam.

Shrines dedicated to Mary, like the one in northern Jordan, can be found throughout the Muslim-majority world. In Egypt, Turkey, Syria, Lebanon, and Israel-Palestine, both Christians and Muslims visit Marian shrines in an act of devotion to her and of worship of God.

In 2010 in Lebanon, Muslim leader Sheikh Mohamad Nokkari brought Muslims and Christians together to celebrate the shared story of Gabriel's appearance to Mary. Now, the feast of the Annunciation is celebrated each year as a national holiday in Lebanon. Muslims and Christians from different traditions, along with their religious leaders, travel to a town called Jamhour to join in song and prayer at a church dedicated to *Sayyidatuna*—Our Lady.[1]

Our journey of interreligious dialogue with Muslims begins with meeting them, learning about their lives, their faith, and what we have in common. In this chapter, I introduce readers to some of the many Muslims I've been blessed to meet and befriend, both in the United States and in the Middle East. Through these relationships, I've come to learn about what Islam means to them—how they understand it and live it out in their daily lives. This picture of Islam I present—painted by roommates, colleagues, shopkeepers, and professors—is supplemented with references to Islamic theology, history, tradition, and scripture that they've shared with me and that I've encountered in my academic study and personal exploration of Islam.

This first chapter also places a strong emphasis on Catholics' similarities with Muslims. Emphasizing our commonalities first, and our differences down the line, is the approach the Catholic Church takes in *Nostra Aetate*, the Second Vatican Council document that speaks about other religions. Rather than focusing on our differences with Muslims, this groundbreaking document, which was released during the 1960s and has shaped the Catholic Church's teaching since then, lingers on what is shared. This approach of beginning with commonalities will help us more quickly develop bonds of friendship and understanding with Muslims that, in turn, will help us grow closer to God.

In this chapter, and throughout the entire book, it is critical for us to remember what the Bible tells us—that every human being is made in God's image and likeness. This truth has no exceptions; it includes the 1.6 billion people in the world who practice the religion of Islam. I've experienced this truth in my own life, thanks to my encounters with Muslims, whether they be strangers or close friends. Countless times, Muslims have revealed God to me. I have seen God at work through their generosity, kindness, courage, and selflessness. In this chapter, I share only a few instances in which I have experienced God through Muslims.

Honoring God by Serving Humanity

The first Muslim I met was Nadir Zaidi. He, like me, attended Brebeuf Jesuit Preparatory School, a Catholic high school run by Jesuit priests in Indianapolis, Indiana. Like many American teens, Nadir was obsessed with NBA basketball, and also aspired to be a doctor. Coincidentally, after graduating from Brebeuf, both of us attended Georgetown University, where Nadir studied biology, taught science to students from marginalized communities, and kept my intermural basketball team afloat with his killer jump shot. After college, Nadir taught seventh grade in Los Angeles through Teach for America, and was named a Los Angeles Lakers "Teacher of the Month."[2] Now, he's a medical student at Cornell, living out his high school dream of becoming a physician.

I vividly remember one seventh-period religion class in high school in which Nadir talked about wanting to become a doctor. He spoke of his desire to perform medicine not just in Carmel, Indiana, where he was from, but also through humanitarian aid missions abroad, perhaps in a place like Pakistan, where his parents were born. "I know people talk about burnout," he said, "but can I really justify not devoting myself fully to helping as many people as possible, regardless of the toll it takes on me?" His passion for helping others struck me, and it challenged me and my classmates to consider how we might help others in our careers. I didn't know a lot about Islam at the time, but I knew that Nadir was a faithful person, and I could see that his passion for helping others flowed from his devotion to God and his religious convictions.

Since meeting Nadir, I've been fortunate to know hundreds of other Muslims, some of whom have become close friends and colleagues, and others of whom simply sold me chewing gum at a corner food mart in Amman. But, nearly all of them have embodied this same spirit of self-giving service I first encountered in Nadir over ten years ago. Kristin, a former colleague and convert to Islam, campaigns to secure paid family leave for workers in Washington, DC. My college roommate, Wardah, now volunteers at a health clinic run by the local Muslim community in New Haven, Connecticut. Even while enrolled in an intense medical program, she plans to run for local office to improve the education system in New Haven. Khalid, a cabdriver I knew in Jordan, once phoned me during a snowstorm to see if I needed a ride to get groceries or to visit friends. When he arrived to pick me up from my apartment, he trudged up the street, took my hand, and helped me down the slippery, snowy hill.

The good works that Muslims do for others are so often an expression of their faith. In their holy text, the Qur'an, Muslims find commands to serve humanity and all of creation, to make a more peaceful and just world where all people can flourish. One scriptural verse often cited as motivation for establishing social justice, even amid difficult circumstances, is this one: "Believers! Be resolute in the doing of justice, as witnesses to God, even though it be against yourselves, your parents or your kinsfolk, and whether it concerns rich or poor. For what has to do with God is more relevant than wealth or poverty. Do not follow your own desires into the perversion of what is right. If you act in bias or prejudice God is well aware of what you are doing" (4:135). A common refrain throughout the Qur'an is about promoting what is good and preventing what is wrong. In one verse, God says, "Let there be a single community of you, sounding the call to good, enjoining what is right and forbidding what is wrong. It is such who truly prosper" (3:104).

The Prophet Muhammad and his community instituted major social reforms in their society of seventh-century Arabia. At that time, the city of Mecca (where Muhammad was born) was marred by sectarian conflict and economic injustice, as well as racial, gender, and social inequality. The injustices of the society, which was dominated by a few wealthy families, were intertwined with a culture of polytheism and idol worship. The Muslim community, led by Muhammad, endeavored to change that. In the Islamic tradition, believing in God is inseparable from doing good works for humanity. The Qur'an constantly pairs monotheism—faith in the one God—with action: "God has promised those who have believed and who practice righteous deeds that forgiveness and a great reward are theirs" (5:9). Another verse instructs, "Worship God and do not elevate anything at all to share His worship. Deal kindly with your parents and your kinsfolk, with orphans and the poor, as well as with the neighbor who is of your kin and the neighbor who is a stranger, with the companion beside you, and with the wayfarer and the slaves in your charge. God does not like the conceited and the boastful" (4:36). In a version of the Golden Rule, the Prophet Muhammad said, "None of you believes unless he wants for his brother what he loves for himself."[3]

Muslims look to the example of the Prophet Muhammad, who they view as the ideal role model for living out God's message. In the Qur'an, God says that he has not sent Muhammad "except as a mercy to the world" (21:107). Muslims strive to live out God's will as Muhammad did—by honoring God through serving humanity. They remember the Prophet as a generous person, always inclined toward forgiveness and gentleness. He was prayerful, extremely frugal, and funny, too. In contradiction to the conceptions many non-Muslims have of him and of the society he helped build, Muhammad's community was built on ideals of equality and religious pluralism, and it remedied many of the injustices that harmed the most vulnerable in seventh-century Arabia.

Muslim individuals, congregations, and communities draw from their faith tradition in carrying out works of service and social justice that extend well beyond their own religious community. Syria Civil Defense, also known as "the White Helmets," is an organization of civilians who attempt to rescue their fellow Syrians harmed in the civil war. Since the beginning of the war in Syria, they have rescued thousands of people from bombed-out buildings in their war-torn country.[4] Concerned with saving as many lives as possible, the group chose a verse from the Qur'an as their motto: "To save a life is to save all of humanity" (5:32).

When numerous African-American churches in the United States were burnt down in 2015, American Muslims raised over $100,000 to help rebuild them. In their efforts, they cited a Qur'anic quote about the importance of protecting churches and houses of worship (22:40).[5] They also cited this one, in which God reminds the Muslim community of their similarities with Christians: "You will find the closest to the believers in affection to be those who say: 'We are Christians,'—the reason being that among them are priests and monks, and they are not a people given to arrogance" (5:82). In a village in Pakistan in 2016, Muslims paid for the rebuilding of a church, which one Muslim contributor called a "house of God."[6] After tombstones belonging to Jewish families were vandalized in St. Louis in 2017, Muslims quickly raised funds to repair them, too. And during the protests in North Dakota against the building of an oil pipeline, Muslims traveled to the Standing Rock Sioux Reservation to express their support for the protests and to give the tribe's leaders holy *Zamzam* water from a well in the holy mosque in Mecca.[7]

In Washington, DC, and London, Muslim-run restaurants serve meals to the homeless on Christmas Day, when many other businesses are closed.[8] Across the United States, Muslims run free health clinics, homeless outreach programs, and shelters for women. As one Milwaukee Muslim put it after delivering aid packages to her city's homeless population, "You don't have to be Muslim to get our help."

This loving spirit of care is also expressed in more subtle, ordinary ways. It is manifested in the dozens of text messages, Facebook messages, and Snapchat videos I have received from Muslim friends like Ayah and Aamir on Christmas. It is contained in the trinkets that friends have brought me from their travels abroad—like the white elephant Aly bought outside the Taj Mahal in India, the flower-petal tea that Aamina brought back for me from Spain, the purse Norbani purchased for me in Indonesia, and the bracelet that Nazir picked up in Rome. This generosity was also contained in the bills and coins my Jordanian cabdriver handed to me after he ran from car to car, and bus to bus, to break my twenty *dinar* bill, so I could get the proper change after our ride through Amman. This kindness was tucked into the packet of cookies that a grandfatherly man with gapped, yellow teeth handed me when I encountered him on the sidewalk on Arar Street, named for the twenty-century Jordanian poet who wrote of Muslim-Christian coexistence.

I saw this hospitality in the friendly, waving gesture of Reema, a mother of four who lives in the green, stone-strewn hillsides of rural Jordan. In the spring of 2012, some American friends and I passed by her home on the outskirts of Amman on our way to visit the ruins of an ancient Jewish castle in the valley. "*Marhaba!* Hello!" I said as we walked by. "*Tafaddili,*" she beckoned from the porch, with her young son on her lap. "Come join us for tea!"

For the next hour, my friends and I talked in broken colloquial Arabic with Reema and her family, sipping gritty coffee and sweet tea under a tangled web of grapevines. Its branches split the sunlight into shards that stretched across her face and that of her husband, Muhammad, whose eyes crinkled in the sunshine as he handed me fresh mint to suck on. All of us sat together, watching their daughter Aseel bounce a blue marble on the floor, and we laughed as baby Ahmed smeared coffee grounds all over his face. When we left and continued down the winding road, nine-year-old Abdullah gave us a snack of unripe almonds as a parting gift. Though the tea and snacks are long gone now, the memory of the family's generous service—and that of so many Muslim friends and strangers—remains one of my most treasured possessions. Their hospitality has been an undeniable expression of God's love for me. Countless times, God has loved me through the Muslims I've met.

The Name of God Is Mercy

Written at the beginning of every chapter of the Qur'an but one, and often recited by Muslims at the start of meals, prayers, and ordinary tasks, is a prayer invoking God's mercy.

The constant reassurance of God's mercy and care is a central aspect of Muslims' faith, and is something I have been struck by in my experiences with Muslims. It comes up frequently in conversations with Muslim friends, in talks I've heard, and in Facebook posts I've read. When asked in a 2016 interview what he wanted more people to understand about his religion, Imam Khalid Latif—a Muslim chaplain for the New York Police Department—talked about mercy. "It's used consistently every day, by every Muslim," he said.[9] Imam Talib Shareef, the head of a Washington, DC, house of worship known as the "Nation's Mosque," says this mercy of God is the "core of Islam."[10] Many Muslims speak of this mercy 230 times throughout the day in prayer.[11]

Similar to the Catholic practice of making the sign of the cross and saying, "In the name of the Father, and the Son, and the Holy Spirit," Muslims recite the phrase, *Bismillah ar-Rahman ar-Rahim*, which can be translated, "In the name of God, the Entirely Merciful, the Always Merciful." This Arabic phrase is used to inaugurate most tasks, especially prayer. *Salah*, a form of prayer most Muslims perform five times daily, combines passages of the Qur'an with movement of the body. It involves standing, bending over, and placing one's forehead on the ground in prostration. *Salah* always includes *Surat al-Fatiha*, the Qur'an's brief opening chapter. This chapter consists of only twenty-nine words in Arabic, but it mentions God's mercy four times:

> In the name of God, the Entirely Merciful, the Always Merciful,
>   Praise be to God, the Cherisher and Sustainer of all being,
> The Entirely Merciful, the Always Merciful,
>   Master of the day of judgment.
>   You alone we worship and You alone we ask for help.
>   Guide us on the straight path,
>   The path of those whom You have blessed,
>   Not of those against whom there is displeasure,
>   Nor of those who go astray.

Surat al-Fatiha plays a central role in Muslim life. The Prophet Muhammad considered this short chapter to contain the whole of the Qur'an's message.[12] *Surat al-Fatiha* is a staple in the prayer life of Muslims to an even greater extent than the Lord's Prayer is for Christians.

Muslims' divine text, the Qur'an, is shorter than the New Testament of the Bible. But the Qur'an uses "mercy" and its related words 339 times.[13] All but one of the Qur'an's chapters starts with the *bismillah* phrase invoking God's mercy. One of the most beloved chapters of the Qur'an is called *ar-Rahman* ("The Entirely Merciful"), which contains a series of reminders of how God's mercy has been manifested to humanity and in creation.

God's mercy comes up elsewhere in the religious life of Muslims, too. The extended version of a common Islamic greeting is "May the peace, mercy, and blessings of God be upon you," and a common prayer upon entering a mosque is "Oh God, open for me the doors of Your mercy." In Arabic, a person who has passed away is referred to as *marhoum*, someone to whom God has shown mercy, and the main Muslim cemetery in Jerusalem is called *Bab ar-Rahma*, "the Gate of Mercy." Mercy is also a frequent motif in Arabic calligraphy, the central form of Islamic artwork that beautifully renders the Qur'an's poetic text into visual art. Mercy has also been a main topic in treatises of Muslim thinkers and poets throughout history, like the medieval philosopher Ibn Arabi, who wrote that God "mercified" the universe into being.[14]

Muslims invoke God's mercy outside of explicitly religious contexts, too. Friends of mine sometimes start exams or essays with the *bismillah* phrase, or will exclaim it when they spill something. I remember my first Arabic teacher, the endearing Dr. Huda, muttering the phrase to herself after accidentally knocking a stack of papers off her desk. This is similar to the practice some Christians have, like writing the acronyms JMJ (for "Jesus, Mary, Joseph") or AMDG (the Latin acronym for the expression, "For the greater glory of God") on the top of school exams.

To more fully understand and appreciate Islam's emphasis on God's mercy, we must learn a bit of Arabic—starting with the word *rahma*. Often translated into English as "mercy," *rahma* has a deeper meaning than this translation conveys. The word comes from the three-letter Arabic root *r-h-m*, which is the basis for the word for a mother's womb, *rahem*. (This is also the word for womb in Hebrew.) In Semitic language and culture, the womb and the insides are the locus of emotion and feeling.[15]

Ar-Rahman and *ar-Rahim*, the two attributes of God used in *Surat al-Fatiha* and throughout the Qur'an, come from this *r-h-m* root and its connection to the womb. *Ar-Rahman* is often translated as "the Compassionate," "the Gracious," or "the Beneficent," but the word means even more than that. I use the translation "the Entirely Merciful" because *ar-Rahman* means one that is *defined* by mercy. *Rahma*—compassion, "feeling with"—is God's very essence. *Ar-Rahim*, the second of these two major attributes, is often translated as "the Always Merciful." *Ar-Rahim* emphasizes that God's mode of interacting with creation is merciful, too; God is always dispensing mercy.

The Prophet Muhammad emphasized the connection between God's mercy and the love of a mother. In a famous *hadith*, or saying, Muhammad tells his followers that God has more mercy toward his servants than a mother does toward her child. On another occasion, Muhammad describes God's mercy as divided into one hundred parts, ninety-nine of which God retained in himself. God bestowed the remaining one one-hundredth upon creation, and "it is because of this [single part] that the mother shows affection to her child and even the beasts and birds show kindness to one another."[16] According to Islamic tradition, God also said to Muhammad, "I am *ar-Rahman*. I created the womb and gave it a name from my own name." Muslims don't refer to God as a parent in the way Christians do; they don't speak of God as "Father." But Islam linguistically links God's mercy to the unconditional love and care that a mother has for the child within her womb.

The Qur'an explicitly identifies *rahma*, which Muslims also translate into English as "loving-kindness," as God's primary quality and essential, defining attribute.[17] Alluding to the caring embrace of a mother, God says of himself in the Qur'an, "My Mercy encompasses all things" (7:156). The Qur'an also says God "proscribed mercy for himself" (6:12) and that the name *ar-Rahman* is synonymous with

Allah, the Arabic word for God (17:110). God also reminds the Prophet to tell the people that God's "mercy prevails" over his wrath.[18] No created thing is outside the realm of God's *rahma*. In the Islamic litany of God's ninety-nine attributes, *ar-Rahman* and *ar-Rahim* head the list.

For Catholics, Islam's focus on God's *rahma* should sound very familiar. Pope Francis has made mercy the cornerstone of his papacy, and he has urged Christians to rediscover the importance of mercy in our faith. From Francis, we hear about God's compassion constantly. It was an especially prominent theme during the Jubilee Year of Mercy, which the pope declared in 2016. For Francis, mercy is more than pity or forgiveness after we've done wrong. It is God's overarching disposition toward his creation, a parental love that extends to all.

In talking about God's mercy, Pope Francis frequently cites Jesus' parable of the Prodigal Son or, as he calls it, the story of the "Merciful Father."[19] In the parable, a young man runs away from his family, abandoning his elderly father and living a life of selfishness. After he squanders his money, he returns with shame to his family home. And, as the Bible tells it, "While [the son] was still a long way off, his father caught sight of him, and was filled with compassion. He ran to his son, embraced him and kissed him" (Luke 15:20).

An oft-cited saying of the Prophet Muhammad reflects a similar picture of God, who is constantly reaching out to humanity: "God says: When a servant of mine draws nearer to Me by the length of a hand, I draw toward him an arm's length; and when he draws near to Me an arm's length, I draw near to him the distance of a wingspan; and if he comes to Me walking, I go to him running."[20]

The Islamic connection between God's mercy and a mother's womb is also present in the Hebrew scriptures of the Bible.[21] In Exodus, God reveals himself to Moses, describing himself using five adjectives in Hebrew, the Semitic language that has many overlapping roots with Arabic. One of the Hebrew adjectives God uses in speaking to Moses is *Rachum*, which, like *Rahman* and *Rahim* in Arabic, indicates the mercy, compassion, and loving embrace of a mother (Exodus 34:6).

To me, the shared emphasis on God's mercy is the strongest and most apparent similarity between Islam and Christianity. The prayers and responsorial psalms Catholics sing in Mass, like "The Lord is Kind and Merciful," mirror similar phrases that come up in Islamic scripture, and the title of the pope's book on mercy, *The Name of God Is Mercy*, strongly resembles the Qur'anic idea. As the Catholic theologian Cardinal Walter Kasper writes in his seminal book on mercy, Christians have understood mercy as God's fundamental attribute from the earliest days of the faith.[22] The same is true for Muslims.

There is a passage from Isaiah that, whenever I hear it, reminds me of Islam's take on God's *rahma*:

> Can a mother forget her infant,
> be without tenderness for the child of her womb?
> Even should she forget,
> I will never forget you. (Isaiah 49:15)

Word Made Flesh

Every Tuesday night during my freshman year at Georgetown, the Muslim chaplain in my dorm opened his apartment and invited in students for tea. After preparing a large pot of sweet chai, Mohammed facilitated conversations about religion for the diverse set of students who would attend his open houses. Conversations about the meaning of fasting, the tension between free will and predestination, and the importance of *nia*, or one's intention, added important layers of learning to the education on Islam I was receiving in the classroom.

It was in the context of Mohammed's open houses that I started to understand that some of my initial conceptions about Islam were incorrect. I had previously assumed that, when comparing Christianity and Islam, it was natural to pair Jesus and the Prophet Muhammad, who were both human beings, and the Bible and the Qur'an, which are both texts. But, as I learned through my conversations with chaplains like Mohammed, and in courses with theology professors like Paul Heck, a Catholic, these central figures and these holy books are not actually equivalents across the two traditions; they serve different roles in the respective religions.

The Qur'an plays a role in Islam like the one Jesus plays in Christianity. For Christians, Jesus is God in our human flesh—*Emmanuel*,

"God with us." The incarnation—God becoming human—is the divine manifesting itself in our created world. We believe that Jesus, as part of the Trinity, has always existed and is the unchanging "Word of God." But we also understand that God became manifest to us in a particular time and place through the flesh-and-blood person of Jesus.

For Muslims, the ultimate manifestation of the divine in creation is the Qur'an. The Qur'an, which means "recitation" or "reading aloud," is God's speech coming into the world. Muhammad called the Qur'an a "rope stretched from Heaven to earth."[23] Muslims believe that God's Word is eternal, preexistent, and unchanging, and yet it entered the created world in the seventh century through a series of revelations to an illiterate man named Muhammad. These revelations were communicated by the angel Gabriel to Muhammad and expressed orally through the Arabic language. Then, they were committed to memory by Muhammad's followers and written down. These verses were sometimes communicated to the Prophet without any clear impetus. But often, they were revealed to address a particular situation or problem the Prophet and his community were dealing with. As Islam scholar Carl Ernst describes, the Qur'an's message centers around belief in the one God, but also on "moral responsibility, the overwhelming creative power of God, and the importance of caring for the poor, widows, and orphans."[24] For Christians and Muslims, respectively, Jesus and the Qur'an are both the unchanging "Word of God," but each also had a specific purpose for the time and place in which it became manifest in the world. In Islam, the revelation of the Qur'an is like the incarnation in Christianity.

If we look closely at the rituals, tradition, and spirituality of Islam, we can understand this theological comparison between the Qur'an and Jesus a bit better. For Muslims, listening to or reciting passages of the Qur'an resembles Catholics' experience of receiving the Eucharist—the Body of Jesus Christ—in Mass. In his podcast, Sheikh Walead Mosaad speaks about how *dhikr*, the practice of recalling God through recitation of Qur'anic verses, allows the Qur'an to become part of one's body, one's flesh and blood.[25] Seyyed Hossein Nasr, a preeminent scholar of Islam, explained at a 2016 conference that reciting the poetry of the Qur'an is "like a piece of heaven in us."[26] In a similar way, when Catholics consume Jesus through the Host at Mass, the divine becomes a part of us. Just as Catholics keep the Eucharist in a sacred box, the tabernacle, in the church, Muslims often place Qur'ans in intricate mother-of-pearl boxes, on wooden stands with geometric designs, or on the highest shelf in their homes. Just as we rush to pick up a consecrated Host and immediately eat it after accidentally dropping it on the floor, Muslims avoid letting their Word of God, the Qur'an, touch the ground.

Mary and Muhammad also have parallel roles in Catholicism and Islam, respectively. Neither are divine, but rather they are sinless, human individuals who live out God's will perfectly. They serve as the vessels through which God's divine Word enters the world. According to Catholic teaching, Mary was born without sin, and in Islamic tradition, Muhammad's heart was scrubbed clean of his sin before he began receiving God's revelations at age forty.[27] Despite the fears that both Mary and Muhammad had about bearing God's Word to humanity, they ultimately said yes and accepted that role. For their decisions to cooperate so fully with God's will, Mary and Muhammad are highly revered, so much so that in some religious contexts Catholics and Muslims have given these human figures an almost divine status. The following figure visually illustrates the respective roles of Jesus and the Qur'an, and Mary and Muhammad:

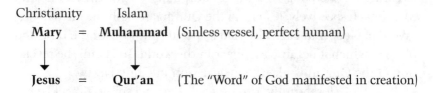

Christianity   Islam

Mary   =   **Muhammad**   (Sinless vessel, perfect human)

Jesus   =   **Qur'an**   (The "Word" of God manifested in creation)

Father Daniel Madigan, a Jesuit priest and expert in Qur'anic studies at Georgetown University, summarizes all of this well in an article about *Nostra Aetate*, the 1965 Vatican II document on the Catholic Church's relationship with other religious traditions:

> For Christians Jesus is not the bearer of the Word of God in the way Muhammad is for Muslims. Rather he *is* that Word, the embodiment of that Word—the "incarnation" we say, the enfleshment of the Word . . . Muslim faith does not claim that Muhammad is the Word, but rather that he is the human

channel through whom the Word entered the world—an Arab prophet to give voice to the Word of God addressed to the Arabs in their own language. In this respect he is a parallel to Mary in the Christian scheme of things—the human person whose cooperation was needed to give flesh to the Word.[28]

As already mentioned, Mary is an important figure for Muslims, too, a role model in the faith. So is Jesus, who also occupies a prominent place in Islam. Jesus, whose Arabic name is Isa in the Qur'an, is viewed by Muslims as a messenger of God's Word, just as Muhammad is. Both men, and other familiar biblical characters like Moses, are understood by Muslims to have been sent by God to deliver a divine message to the world and to bring humanity back to "the straight path" of right belief and action. In the Qur'anic revelations, God emphasizes that both Muhammad and Jesus are *human* bearers of God's revelation. In Islam, neither are seen as divine, but both men play extraordinarily important roles. Sent as "mercies to the world," the Qur'an says, both men conveyed God's message to humanity and performed miracles through God's power. Islamic tradition contains beautiful, miraculous stories about Jesus—like when, as a baby, he spoke up to defend his mother against charges of infidelity, and when as an adult healed the sick and transformed a clay bird into a living one.

As the important role of Jesus in Islam suggests, Muslims do not believe that their religion started with Muhammad. Rather, the message that Muhammad brought six centuries after Jesus was the same one brought by Jesus and many throughout history before him. These prophets include Adam, Noah, Abraham, Isaac, David, and John the Baptist, whose stories are told or referenced in the Qur'an. Muhammad is understood as the "seal of the Prophets," the last of these messengers to convey God's eternal revelation and to bring humanity back to the religion professed by all of these holy figures (Qur'an 3:84). While Muhammad is seen as the epitome of a prophet of God and as a perfect human, all of these figures are revered and considered models in the faith.

The Image of God

The picture of Muslims and their religion that I have painted in this chapter is quite different than the one many of us might be used to seeing in the media. It is colored by notions of social justice and mercy, and is replete with familiar characters from our own Christian scripture. This image of Islam may be unfamiliar, but it is the one the Catholic Church wants us to see.

The Vatican II declaration on other religions, *Nostra Aetate*, tells its readers that the Catholic Church holds Muslims in "high regard" (3). It goes on to describe core aspects of Muslims' faith, many of which are things that relate to or are shared with Christianity:

> They worship God, who is one, living and subsistent, merciful and almighty, the Creator of heaven and earth, who has also spoken to humanity. They endeavor to submit themselves without reserve to the hidden decrees of God, just as Abraham submitted himself to God's plan, to whose faith Muslims eagerly link their own. Although not acknowledging him as God, they venerate Jesus as a prophet; his virgin Mother they also honor, and even at times devoutly invoke. Further, they await the day of judgment and the reward of God following the resurrection of the dead. For this reason they highly esteem an upright life and worship God, especially by way of prayer, alms-deeds and fasting.[29]

There is much we Christians share with Muslims, and these similarities help form the basis of our relationships with Muslims.

Of course, our similarities extend beyond religious matters, too. (I'll elaborate further on some of these similarities in chapter 2.) Like my family back home in Indiana, many of my Muslim friends are big basketball fans. Youth leagues organized by mosques in Indiana are a big deal, and during March Madness or the NBA tournament my Facebook feed is often flooded with Muslim friends posting about the games. As a native of the Midwestern state where basketball is revered above all other sports, I grew up around the game and played it competitively for years. But my love for this quintessentially Indiana sport pales in comparison to that of my Muslim friends.

Every year, the Catholic and Jesuit high school that I attended in Indianapolis gives what is called the Saint of God Award. It is bestowed on a member of the senior class who gives one's life to others, lives out one's religion, and exemplifies a spirit of saintliness. When my class graduated, the award was given to my friend Nadir.

In Christianity, we often talk about how each person is created in God's image and likeness. In Islam, Muslims speak of how God's breath, or spirit, resides in each person.[30] In getting to know Muslims like Nadir, I have encountered God's image and spirit in Muslims countless times. Muslim friends and strangers have revealed God to me through their embodiment of the virtues of generosity, hospitality, and self-sacrifice. In their living out ordinary lives—but with passion to establish justice and goodness in the world—I've seen God at work. Interreligious dialogue offers each of us this blessing of meeting Muslims, and of meeting God in them, too.

2

What We Fear,
and Who Gets Hurt

We cannot truly pray to God the Father of all if we treat any people as other than sisters and brothers, for all are created in God's image.

—Second Vatican Council, *Nostra Aetate* (5)

Imagine that you're sitting in Mass with your family during Advent. It's an exciting time of year—almost Christmas—and the parish community is excitedly anticipating the upcoming holiday. During the sign of peace, you wave to your friend across the crowded sanctuary, and shake hands with the fidgety kids sitting in the row behind you. You greet another friend and ask how meal preparations are going for dinner with her relatives who just came into town.

Suddenly, the congregation breaks out in gasps. Amid the confusion, you learn that someone outside is shooting a gun at the building. There are children outside, but miraculously, no one is injured.

This story isn't imaginary. In 2012, worshipers at a Chicago-area mosque were gathered for congregational *salah* prayer during Ramadan, the holy season of fasting, prayer, and festive community gatherings. A man approached their mosque with a pellet gun and shot the building during a packed service while hundreds of people were inside.[1]

Imagine what that would be like. Imagine, too, that this attack on your house of worship is not an isolated incident; dozens of other churches have been targeted. People have vandalized them with vulgar language, forced their way inside and desecrated the Eucharist, or even bombed sanctuaries and set them on fire. Parishioners have been assaulted and even killed as they arrive for or leave church services during Christmastime. On social media, you have heard about incidents of harassment that your fellow Catholics have experienced at the grocery store or walking in the park. Your children, or those of your friends, come home from school with stories of being bullied for being Catholic.

When your religion comes up in the news, it is usually juxtaposed with images of violence. Violent criminals who maim and kill are always reported as "Christian militants," while ordinary people like you and your family, who find your faith to be a source of goodness, are rarely featured in headlines. At the same time, politicians claim that your religion motivates violence and oppression. During election campaigning, some of them vow to ban Catholics from the country. Then, when these politicians are in office, they enact policies that attempt to do just that. Regardless of the political party in power, you know that the government and police are keeping a special eye on your community, not just at airports but also at churches and restaurants owned by your relatives. You do your best to go about your day-to-day life normally, but all of this is in the back of your mind.

For Muslims living in the United States, as well as in Europe and elsewhere, this is not an imaginative exercise. It is often reality. In the years before and since the Chicago mosque attack, people who are Muslim (or who are perceived to be) have faced prejudice, discrimination, and even violence. People who I know and care about have been hurt in these sorts of incidents. During college, my friend Muneeb's hometown mosque in Ohio was burned down in arson. Aamina, a young woman I worked with who wears a headscarf, was cursed at as she walked home in downtown Washington, DC, in 2015. My colleague and friend Nazir lost his uncle when he was shot and killed in a Seattle hate crime.

This chapter is about anti-Muslim prejudice and how we, as Christians, are connected to it. In the coming pages, I show how Islamophobia impacts the lives of many American Muslims, and how it is similar to the anti-Catholic discrimination and biases of earlier American generations. I also discuss the importance of acknowledging our own biases toward Muslims. Few of us are immune from this kind of implicit bias; we all carry stereotypes and assumptions about people who are different from us. There have been moments when my own preconceived notions about Muslims have caused me to have a negative view of others or treat them unfairly, even if unintentionally. At times, I've allowed prejudice to pass by unchecked, and I've been reluctant to speak up upon hearing a family member or friend make a comment about Muslims that I know is untrue or unkind. In the coming pages, I look back on some of the ways my own misconceptions about Muslims have been broken down through personal experiences and education.

We cannot hope to build meaningful relationships with Muslims—and with God—if we ignore another's suffering and if we fail to examine our role in it. It is important that we as Christians are witnesses to the prejudice and discrimination our Muslim friends face, and that we grapple with the stereotypes we hold on to. In his apostolic exhortation The Joy of the Gospel, Pope Francis said that our respect for Muslims "should lead us to avoid hateful generalisations."[2] I hope this chapter can help us live up to Francis's call and more readily embrace Muslims as friends.

Similar Stereotypes

In the spring of 1844, several Catholic churches were set on fire during anti-Catholic riots in Philadelphia. Anti-Catholic prejudice had been present in the United States since its founding, but the arrival of Catholic immigrants from Ireland and Germany inflamed this prejudicial sentiment that sometimes erupted into violence.[3]

The Protestant-majority public feared that Catholics were coming to the United States to change its culture and way of life. Catholics were viewed as religious outsiders, who would be more devoted to the pope than they were to the US Constitution. There were conspiracy theories that Catholics were infiltrating the education system and other institutions with the goal of taking over and instituting their foreign religious law. During this time, anti-Catholic cartoons portrayed Irish immigrants as monkey-like drunks and priests as sexually deviant oppressors of nuns. In one newspaper cartoon by Thomas Nast titled *The American River Ganges*, Catholic bishops were depicted as crocodiles coming ashore to attack American schoolchildren.[4] By the 1850s, a political party, called the "American Party" but better known today as the "Know-Nothings," was formed to capitalize politically on anti-Catholic fears. Italians and Catholics of other nationalities also faced similar hostilities when they immigrated to the United States.

Today, down the street from St. Michael's Catholic Church, one of the churches torched in the anti-Catholic riots in Philadelphia, sits Al-Aqsa Islamic Society, a mosque belonging to the city's Muslim community.[5] In December 2015, a severed pig's head was thrown at the entrance to the mosque, and the leadership has received hateful phone messages, too.

The anti-Muslim prejudice that exists today in many ways resembles the anti-Catholic discrimination of the past. Today's news and entertainment media often depict Muslims using stereotypes that were once used to characterize Catholics: foreign, dangerous, and intent on subverting American law to institute Islamic law. Lies about Muslims are conveyed not through nineteenth-century political cartoons but memes that circulate on social media.

In the 1850s, a member of the Know-Nothing Party and a representative in Congress, Thomas R. Whitney, wrote a popular book called *A Defence of the American Policy*, where he wrote of a supposed Catholic conspiracy to take over America. The "subtle" yet "insidious" Jesuits, he wrote, are intent on converting America into "a papal nation and government."[6] These claims, which sound almost humorous to us today, were a way people justified their biases and even mistreatment of Catholics during that period. In our current time, people claim (without basis) that Muslims have a plan of "stealth *jihad*" to usurp American law in favor of *sharia*, which is portrayed (inaccurately) as an unchanging system of Islamic law that centers on brutal punishments.

Amid these contemporary concerns about Muslims, American mosques have faced a similar fate to Philadelphia's Catholic churches in the 1840s. In recent years, people have broken into mosques and ripped up Qur'ans, spray-painted vulgar language on the exterior of buildings, shot bullets into signs, and left pig heads, bacon, and even feces on the property. In 2017, worshipers at a Minnesota mosque were miraculously not harmed when a firebomb was thrown into a window, and in Florida a man slammed his car into several cars parked outside an Islamic center. Militia groups have held demonstrations outside of mosques, with participants carrying automatic firearms. Mosques around the country have also received hateful letters and phone messages threatening violence, and their congregants have been beaten up and murdered coming and going from liturgies during Ramadan. In many places throughout the United States, Muslim communities hoping to build or renovate mosques have faced opposition from locals who fear that Muslims want to use the space to indoctrinate youth and plan violent attacks.

After the Philadelphia Al-Aqsa mosque was desecrated, people from all over the city gathered for a potluck meal to express their support for the Muslim community. A few weeks later at an interfaith gathering to beautify the mosque, Philadelphia mayor Jim Kenney, a Catholic, emphasized that fear of the "other" was at the root of both the anti-Catholic sentiment of the past and the anti-Muslim feelings of today. "Those three churches were burned to the ground with the same type of attitude . . . that is permeating the country today in this national conversation [about Muslims]," he said.[7]

The Consequences of Fear

On a Wednesday afternoon, when I was working as a researcher at the Bridge Initiative at Georgetown, one of my interns poked her head into my office. This was strange; Naaz didn't usually come in on Wednesdays. But before I could say hello, Naaz burst into tears. I stood up, gave her a hug, and for several seconds she cried into my shoulder. This was the day after the 2016 presidential election, and Naaz—like many Muslims—felt afraid.

During the presidential campaign, some candidates proposed measures that would explicitly discriminate against Muslims based on their religion. In December 2015, then-candidate Donald Trump called for the "total and complete shutdown of Muslims" entering the country.[8] Even as this proposal became more watered down as the election campaign moved forward, my Muslim friends were understandably concerned. Policies that discriminate against people because of their religion, national origin, and ethnicity have been enacted in the United States before, especially during times of conflict or war. In the wake of the attack on Pearl Harbor in 1941 President Franklin D. Roosevelt declared war on Japan and issued an executive order to round up Japanese Americans. US citizens of Japanese heritage were thought to be a threat to the country, and were held prisoner for years in internment camps in the American West. The internment of Japanese Americans during World War II is a reminder that wars abroad can lead to the scapegoating of entire communities and even to the infringement of citizens' rights that should be protected by the US Constitution.[9]

For Muslims, discrimination at the hands of government and law enforcement isn't only hypothetical. During the presidencies of George W. Bush and Barack Obama, American Muslims were surveilled at their houses of worship and local restaurants, and profiled at airports. Under a program with the acronym NSEERS, immigrants from numerous Muslim-majority countries were required to register with the government.[10] Ordinary American Muslims have found themselves interrogated by law enforcement and entered into a counterterrorism database for engaging in perfectly normal activities, like buying computers or taking photos of famous landmarks.[11]

Knowing this history of discrimination against Japanese Americans and Muslims—not to mention other groups—it's no surprise that Naaz was concerned after election day in 2016. The winning candidate had, more than once, expressed his belief that there is a "problem" in the Muslim community, and he had called for surveillance at mosques and even shutting some down. Just a week after his inauguration, President Donald Trump signed an executive order targeting Muslims and Syrian refugees, a version of which later went into effect pending review by the US Supreme Court. The order strikingly resembled the immigration restrictions preventing Jewish refugee resettlement during World War II. Then, amid high anti-Semitism and concerns that Nazis would sneak into the United States along with Jews fleeing the Holocaust, the US decided to turn many European Jews away before and during the war.[12]

These episodes of discrimination in American history are ones we'd rather forget. But if we don't acknowledge these past wrongs, we run the risk of also failing to recognize their modern-day manifestations. Catholics, Japanese, and Jews were once the groups viewed as foreign. They were often blamed for problems, cast as dangerous by the media and politicians, and perceived as a group that would always be "other," never part of "us." Today, Muslims are that group. The nightly news and our social media often show Muslims as terrorists, not as ordinary people. Websites and cable channels claim that refugees from Syria will be infiltrated by violent fighters who aim to harm our country. When acts of violence are committed by people who claim the religion of Islam, it is portrayed as the norm (not the exception) within the religion—despite the fact that virtually all Muslims see their religion as a source of goodness and peace, and live it out that way.

In the days after Naaz came, tearful, into my office, my colleagues and I heard what felt like countless news reports and stories on social media of American Muslims being harassed or assaulted. And throughout my time working at the Bridge Initiative on Islamophobia, I saw how prejudice and discrimination touch Muslims in their daily lives. Muslim parents have come home to find their houses vandalized or dotted with bullet holes. A mother in North Carolina was injured when an unknown perpetrator shot into her home while she, her husband, and kids were sleeping inside. Women who wear headscarves have been physically assaulted while out on walks with their children. Men who sport beards, wear traditional clothing, or speak foreign languages have been beaten up and been doused with hot coffee by passersby. Some anti-Muslim incidents have been deadly. In 2015, Yusor Abu-Salha, her husband Deah Barakat, and her little sister Razan were brutally killed in their home in Chapel Hill, North Carolina, by a neighbor who had intimidated them before and harbored antireligious sentiment. That year, the FBI documented the highest number of anti-Muslim hate crimes since 2001, the year of the September 11th attacks.[13] Many of them involved physical violence. As of this writing, the hate crime statistics for 2016 and 2017 have yet to be released, but analysts anticipate that the numbers of Islamophobic crimes will remain high. And these statistics will not necessarily include many incidents in which Muslims have been harmed or killed in attacks with unclear motives.

Those who aren't Muslim have also been harmed by anti-Muslim sentiment. When a man charged into a Sikh gurdwara in Oak Creek, Wisconsin, and killed six people in 2012, he thought the congregants were Muslim. Often, anti-Muslim bias is wrapped up in other forms of cultural and racial bias. Being Muslim, Arab, or Middle Eastern—or simply having brown skin—are often indistinguishable to many Americans who don't come from these backgrounds. But these identities are distinct and shouldn't be conflated; there are many Arabs who aren't Muslim, for example. (See glossary for further elaboration.) Shortly after September 11, 2001, a man who wanted to "kill a Muslim" gunned down Balbir Singh Sodhi, a Sikh man who wore a turban.[14] In 2016, Arab-American Christian Khalid Jabara was killed by a neighbor who had used a number of racist slurs, including anti-Muslim ones, against the Jabara family.[15] Srinivas Kuchibohtla, a man from India, was shot and killed in a Kansas Applebee's in 2017 because the alleged perpetrator thought his brown skin meant he was from the Middle East, a geographical region distinct from India and other South Asian countries.[16] All of this is why Islamophobia is often discussed as a form of racism. People who "look Muslim" but who aren't are still at risk from bias incidents motivated by anti-Muslim sentiment, while Muslims who don't have brown skin or who don't wear distinctive clothing face little bias until they tell people they're Muslim.

Even when Islamophobia isn't manifested as physical violence, it still causes harm. While running the New York City Marathon and attending a Spurs basketball game with his dad, my Sikh friend Simran was called anti-Muslim slurs. Muslim friends who wear headscarves have been yelled at and told to "go home." They have had to get used to snide remarks, suspicious stares, and constant questions like "where are you from?" even though New Jersey, Texas, or Indiana is their home. Subtle prejudices like these weigh on a person. Children are impacted, too. Many Muslim children have been called "terrorist," "Osama," or "ISIS" by fellow students, and in some cases bullied by their teachers. A woman I know through Facebook, Asima, told me a story about her young son's interaction

with a classmate after election day in 2016. The student started list-
ing the groups of people he had secretly disliked, and whom he now
thought the new president would send out of the country: Muslims,
Latinos, and other minority groups. Asima's son was so troubled by
the comment that he threw up and had to be taken home. A 2017
survey found that half of US Muslims had experienced at least one
instance of religious discrimination in the past year.[17]

When we hear prejudicial rhetoric about Muslims from our politicians, learn of cases of discrimination at airports, or read statistics
about hate crimes in news articles online, we can see that Islamophobia is clearly a problem. But it can often seem like an abstract
issue with few consequences if those facts aren't coupled with examples of how Islamophobia impinges on the lives of Muslims and
others. Anti-Muslim prejudice and discrimination seriously impact
the daily lives of human beings—friends and neighbors, parents and
grandparents, young adults and children—who simply want to live
a safe and fulfilled life dedicated to family, to God, and to making
the world a better place.

Fruit Sellers or Firebrands?

When studying abroad in Jordan, I lived with a host family in
the capital, Amman. One afternoon, while I was sitting on my bed,
I heard a loud voice echoing through a megaphone outside. Only a
couple of weeks into my study abroad experience, I was startled by a
man's garbled Arabic speech and his rushed, emphatic tone. *Is that
a political agitator?* I wondered. *He sounds angry. Is he calling his
fellow Jordanians to rise up?* After all, it was early 2012, and protests
inspired by the Arab Spring were still common in Jordan.

"*Meen hooweh?* Who is that?" I asked my host mother, who was
walking past the door to the bedroom I shared with my host sister.
"Oh, that's only the fruit seller," she said.

I would later learn that it's common in Amman, Jordan, and
elsewhere in the Middle East, for fruit and vegetable vendors to sell
their produce out of a pickup truck, driving through neighborhoods
and advertising their sales through a prerecorded message projected
through a loudspeaker. As I got more comfortable with the Arabic

dialect spoken in Jordan, I began to understand the produce trucks' megaphone messages:

"Yullah bandora, yullah bandora! Baitinjaan, koosa! Yullah batata, yullah batata!" "Come get your tomatoes! Eggplant and zucchini! We've got potatoes! Come get your potatoes!"

After learning the real purpose and meaning behind the loud voice outside, I felt embarrassed about my initial reaction to the fruit vendor's shouting. It brought into clear relief my own assumptions and stereotypes about people who live in the Middle East. I had assumed that the man was angry, potentially dangerous, and intent on political or religious upheaval.

It's not surprising that I had these stereotypes. For my entire life, I—like virtually all Americans—had been bombarded with news and images on TV that almost always presented Muslims in the context of war and violent political change. The nightly news had never shown Muslims yelling to sell fruits and vegetables; it had only shown Muslims yelling while launching rockets or protesting in the streets.

My decision to study abroad in the Middle East during college was born out of my desire to help break down stereotypes about Muslims back home in the United States. But this experience revealed to me that I still had my own implicit biases to overcome. My interactions with Muslims over the past several years, both in the United States and abroad, have prompted numerous moments like this one I had in Jordan—realizations about the biases that I still hold and must continue to dismantle, both in myself and in my community.

One of the most enduring stereotypes about Muslims is that their religion encourages violence. On social media, we see memes with Qur'anic quotes that seem to call for indiscriminate violence against those of other faiths. Best-selling authors and television personalities portray the Prophet Muhammad as a bloodthirsty warlord whose violence Muslims are compelled to emulate. These notions are also confirmed in news media, which always seems filled with reports of militant groups with Arabic-sounding names whose complex motives are often reduced to simplistic explanations of religion. This narrative about Muslims and violence isn't a new one. Since Europeans' earliest encounters with Islam centuries ago, European literature and visual art has portrayed Muslims as uniquely barbaric and warring.

What does the Islamic tradition say about violence and *jihad*, and what do Muslims actually believe? The truth is that Islam strongly values the human dignity of each person, as God's attentive care for human beings is often mentioned in the Qur'an (see more in chapter 4). The preservation and protection of human life is at the core of Islam's moral and ethical teaching. Muslims often cite this passage of the Qur'an (which is a direct paraphrase of the Jewish Talmud) to illustrate the value of human life: "If a person kills another human soul . . . it would be as if he killed all of humanity. And if a person saves one soul, it is as if he saved all of humanity" (Qur'an 5:32).

Contrary to many Americans' expectations, *jihad* doesn't mean an all-out aggressive war against non-Muslims. Like the word "crusade," *jihad* has multiple meanings. In a saying, or *hadith*, often cited by Muslims, the Prophet Muhammad spoke about two types of *jihad*: the "lesser" and the "greater." This lesser *jihad*, which concerns fighting, can be compared to Christianity's framework for "just war." It has strict conditions and rules: violence can only be waged to defend against an aggressor who is harming an innocent party; it must be proportional; and it must cease once the aggression has let up. The harming of innocents, particularly children and the elderly, can never be justified, and houses of worship—including churches, synagogues, and mosques—should be protected.[18] The Prophet Muhammad's own sayings prohibit killing women, children, elderly, monks, and rabbis, as well as cutting down trees and poisoning water wells. Today, and as in other contexts throughout history, there are violent groups and armies engaging in aggression that have used the word *jihad* to describe their violence. But they do so while eschewing the Islamic requirements and teachings. In an online letter addressed to Abu Bakr al-Baghdadi, the leader of ISIS, over a hundred Muslim scholars from around the world methodically laid out how the brutality of the so-called Islamic State is in total opposition to Islamic teachings.[19]

Though *jihad* is sometimes used in reference to violence, most Muslims today use *jihad* to describe their personal struggles in trying to live a life pleasing to God. *Jihad* literally means "struggle" or "effort," and for the Prophet Muhammad, the struggle to improve oneself was the more noble, "greater *jihad*." This idea of struggling against the self is common in Christianity, too. In Arabic translations of the New

Testament, the verbs related to *jihad* are used to describe the exertion and effort that goes into following God. (Arabic-speaking Christians even name their children Jihad!) When groups like ISIS use the word *jihad* in an attempt to justify their actions using religion, they betray the meanings of both the "lesser" and "greater" *jihad*.

Even if we can accept that violence and terrorism are contrary to Islamic teaching and norms, we still may be left wondering why it seems that so many Muslims around the world engage in violence out of apparent religious convictions. But this perception is not a reflection of reality, for at least two reasons. First, virtually all of the world's 1.6 billion Muslims have not engaged in violence, joined a militant group, or committed an act of terrorism. Muslims, like ordinary people everywhere, go about typical lives that don't usually make it into the news. But, because violence sells, Muslims who engage in war and violence appear more regularly in our news feeds, far exceeding their proportion in the Muslim population. Additionally, a 2017 study found that Muslim perpetrators of violence receive more media airtime than non-Muslim perpetrators.[20] The media's bombardment of stories about Muslims and violence makes us more fearful than we need to be.

Second, we must remember that people are motivated to do harmful things to others for complex and varied reasons. They might have political or social aims, be seeking identity or purpose, be operating out of a state of desperation or duress, or even have mental health challenges. Religion sometimes becomes a way to justify or make sense of these motives. People who join ISIS might cherry-pick verses of the Qur'an in an attempt to justify their actions, or they may invoke God when harming another person. But in the process, they also abandoned the bulk of the Islamic tradition, including its highest ideals.

In the summer of 2016, during an in-flight interview with journalists, Pope Francis declared, "I believe that it's not fair to identify Islam with violence. It's not fair and it's not true."[21] He understood that it wasn't fair to conflate Islam with terrorism, and pointed to the many instances of violence committed by Catholics that aren't attributed to their religion.

But despite the facts and the urging of Pope Francis, the narrative about Islam and violence is hard to shake, so much so that even those of us who actively want to dismantle our biases have a difficult time doing so. Even when we inform ourselves of facts, and form relationships with Muslims, stereotypes can continue to show up. It's embarrassing to admit, but even while writing this book I've been confronted by this stereotype about Muslims and violence in myself. There have been times in Washington, DC's subway system where I've seen a brown-skinned man with a beard and a big backpack, and have found my mind wondering if he might have an explosive. I know that this initial reaction is wrong, and realize it's the result of the power of implicit biases. I don't know if this bias will ever fully go away, but I know that the process of acknowledging and being honest about it will help keep me on the path to overcoming these latent, yet powerful, fears.

Hesitant about Headscarves

On a bright, sunny morning in central Jerusalem, an American friend and I approached a domed house of worship. A sign outside the door asked us to remove our shoes, so we slipped off our sandals and walked inside. A woman wearing a long floral skirt and a sweeping white headscarf bowed and prostrated in prayer, her forehead and lips touching the elaborate carpets covering the floors. If it weren't for the icons and crucifixes on the walls, I would have thought I was visiting a mosque. But this place was an Ethiopian Orthodox church, and the woman in the white scarf was Christian. Later that year, when I visited churches in rural Jordan, like one at Jesus' baptismal site along the Jordan River, I saw Christian women who, outside of a church setting, I would have guessed were Muslim. They wore long black dresses and headscarves just like their Muslim counterparts who lived in the countryside.

These experiences were, for me, a reminder that Muslim women's way of covering their hair with a scarf has resonances in my own religious tradition. Many of my fellow Christians wear a scarf or mantilla during Mass, and Jesus' mother, Mary, dons a headscarf in almost every painting or statue she's depicted in.

Despite the fact that covering one's head in worship is a common practice in Christianity, many Christians in Europe and North

America, including myself, still grapple with stereotypes about Islam and women, especially when it comes to headscarves. To some, the *hijab* is evidence that Muslim women aren't free, that they are oppressed in some way by the piece of cloth many wear on their heads.

The notion that "Islam oppresses women" is, like the stereotype about Muslims being violent, a deep-seated one in Western culture. For generations, operas, plays, literature, and television have advanced the stereotype that Muslim men have a penchant for mistreating women. We assume that Muslims' religion, Islam, is the source of the lack of freedom and inequality we perceive.

This perception of Islam as the cause of widespread oppression of women is not an accurate one. Though it might be surprising to many Christians, Muslims find in their religion a strong emphasis on women's empowerment and rights. The Qur'an emphasizes the equality of all people before God, whether they be male or female, free or enslaved people, or of various races. Guided by God's revelation to create a more just society, the Prophet Muhammad's community sought to elevate women's status, and right many of the wrongs against women that existed in seventh-century Arabia. In contradiction to the Arab customs of the time, the Qur'an and the Muslim community gave women rights in contracting their own marriages and to initiate divorce. The Prophet's community also gave women inheritance rights and property ownership—things that women in Europe would not be granted by men until the 1800s. Muslims point to Khadija, the Prophet's wife and the first Muslim, Mary, the mother of Jesus, and countless others as examples of empowered females in their tradition.

Like Christians and Jews, Muslims have diverse ideas about how the equality of men and women before God is expressed in social and religious life. Muslim women throughout history have occupied powerful roles, serving their communities as leaders, scholars, poets, warriors, and mothers. The Prophet Muhammad is known to have said that "heaven lies under the feet of one's mother." Muslim-majority societies haven't always lived up to Islam's ideals about the treatment of women. But as we are all well aware, this is not simply a problem found in Muslim-majority contexts. Societies that are primarily Christian also have deep-seated histories of women's inequality.

When we realize this, our stereotypes about Muslim women as uniquely oppressed begin to fall away. Furthermore, many Muslim women's rights activists use Islam and Qur'an-based arguments to point out contradictions between the laws, policies, and norms in some Muslim-majority countries and Islamic religious values.

Most Muslim women wear a scarf while praying *salah*, as some Christian women around the world do when in church. Many Muslim women I know wear headscarves in public when in the presence of males who aren't their family members. No woman I know is forced to wear it; in fact, many have chosen to wear it against the wishes of their parents. Some wear it because it's the common practice in the society in which they live, or because they believe Islam dictates the practice. Some also choose to wear it because it enhances their relationship with God by constantly reminding them that they are always in God's presence.

Many Muslim women see the headscarf as an expression not only of their religious identity, but also as a source of empowerment. Despite their diverse reasons for donning the scarf, these Muslim women understand that a woman's freedom and agency is not simply bound up in the act of removing clothing or displaying her body. Rather, they believe modest dressing is something that can give a woman the power not to be defined by her body or appearance. Thus, many Muslim women—even those who don't wear a headscarf—adopt a practice of modesty in appearance. The word *hijab*, though often used to describe the scarf worn on the head, actually encapsulates this broader ethic of modesty or "covering." Physical modesty for both men and women is instructed by God in the Qur'an.

In the West, showing skin is often tied to notions of women's liberation. But does it have to be? Modesty, too, can be empowering. Just ask many Catholic sisters who wear habits and cover their hair. Neither exposing nor covering parts of one's body is an inherently liberating act; it's about having the freedom that allows a person to best live out the life of devotion and service to which God is calling her.

I have worn a *hijab* many times, usually in the context of Islamic prayer or while in a mosque. I did not wear one in public when I lived in Jordan and was never pressured to. Contrary to popular belief, there is wide diversity in what women wear in Muslim-majority countries. Even in Jordan, Muslim women's dress ranges from a T-shirt and jeans to a face veil and long coat. When I have worn a headscarf, especially when I wore it for a full day in Washington, DC, in 2016, I felt like myself. I didn't feel oppressed by the cloth on my head, but did notice that some strangers interacted with me differently than I was used to.

Despite this knowledge and these experiences, I find that sometimes stereotypes still arise in me when I encounter someone who wears a *hijab*. Though I hardly notice a headscarf on friends and colleagues I've known for a while, I still have to check my internal preconceptions when I meet someone new. Like with the stereotype about violence, confronting this bias in myself is not a pleasant realization. But naming it and then working to let it go is a positive step.

Conflict or Coexistence?

Every few weeks on Facebook or Twitter, I receive comments from people I don't know, responding to content I've shared and saying something to this effect: "As a Christian, you could never be allowed to practice your faith in a Muslim country. Islam tells Muslims not to tolerate other religions." What those who leave these comments don't realize is that I have lived very openly as a Christian in a Middle Eastern, Muslim-majority country. Social media posts like this emerge from another enduring stereotype that warrants discussion—that Muslims are instructed by their religion to be hostile toward those of other faiths. This trope flies in the face of both the reality on the ground in Muslim-majority societies, and of Islamic teachings on other religions.

I lived in Amman, Jordan, for over a year in total. There are few places—including in the United States—where I have felt more comfortable visibly proclaiming my Christian faith. In Jordan, I often walked around with a rosary bracelet around my wrist, or an olive wood cross on a black thread around my neck.

Taxi drivers often asked me about my religion. "I'm Christian," I'd answer in Arabic, adding, "*Al-kanisa al-latinia*" to indicate my affiliation with the Roman Catholic Church. Once, a driver pointed to his Islamic prayer beads hanging from his rearview mirror. "Ah yes," he said, "you Christians have your rosary just like we have our *masbaha*." Many cabdrivers I encountered also hung their prayer beads on the mirror, or placed a small Qur'an on the dash, just as Christians do with their rosaries. "We Muslims respect all the religions because we believe in all the heavenly books," the driver said. He was referring to the fact that Muslims believe their religion is, along with Judaism and Christianity, part of the Abrahamic family of religions. Rather than a wholly distinct set of beliefs or a departure from past religions, Islam is understood as a culmination of previous revelation given to Moses and Jesus in the Torah and in the Gospels, respectively.

I had countless conversations like this one with other cabdrivers and shopkeepers while living in Amman. Only on the rarest occasions did I meet someone who expressed hope that I would convert to Islam. And, to the surprise of the strangers who pester me on Twitter, these comments from cabdrivers remained just that: statements of encouragement to explore Islam further, or arguments of persuasion. I assured these few people that I in fact love their religion, and that it has taught me much (something I'll elaborate on more in the coming chapters).

Far more often in Jordan, my conversations resembled one I had with a man named Khadr, the Muslim caretaker of the ancient Church of the Apostles in the town of Madaba. He toured me and my friends around the site, where colorful mosaics—more than fifteen hundred years old—are still largely intact. When I asked him about Muslim-Christian relations in Jordan, which was the topic of my research when I lived there on a Fulbright grant, he said in Arabic, "We Muslims and Christians are like siblings, praise be to God. We have one religion: prayer and worship, *Alhamdulillah*."

In the Qur'an, God praises the diversity of humankind and says to all people, "Humanity! Truly We [God] created you male and female and made you to be nations and tribes in order that you might get to know each other. Truly the noblest among you in God's sight are those who are most mindful of Him. God is the All-Knowing and is Well-Acquainted with all things" (49:13). God explains that our human diversity is intentional, and that our distinct differences are actually a means to connect with one another. Instead of arguing over religion, God says, people of different faiths should "compete" with each other by doing good works: "Had God so willed He could have made you a single community. However He has willed to put you to the test respecting the revelation brought to you. Strive to excel in good things. All of you will return to God, when He will inform you about the things over which you differed" (5:48). The Qur'an also contains what many consider the clearest statement about freedom of religion in any religious scripture. The brief statement "let there be no compulsion in religion" (2:256) is often cited by Muslims as evidence for Islam's support for religious freedom. The Qur'an also speaks to the salvation of non-Muslims. In a number of places in the holy scripture, God reassures its listeners that all those who are devoted to God and do good works have no need to fear about the afterlife (2:62; 2:112; 5:69). Two of these verses specifically mention Christians and Jews.

Support for religious diversity and freedom was built into the earliest Islamic community in the city of Medina, where Muhammad and his followers fled after facing harsh persecution at the hands of the powerful leaders of Mecca. Muhammad was asked by the residents of Medina to be the arbiter of a dispute and lead the diverse community there. This resulted in a covenant or pact, often referred to as "the Constitution of Medina." It acknowledged that the Jews and Muslims of the city were one community, or *umma*. As Islam scholar Jonathan Brown notes in his biography of Muhammad, the Jewish residents of the city were "guaranteed the same rights and security as Muslims" and practiced their religion freely.[22]

Large populations of Jews and Christians have lived and flourished in Muslim-majority societies since the time of the Prophet. In general, the Muslim world was more tolerant of religious diversity than Christian Europe.[23] Even in later contexts where non-Muslims had different rights and duties from Muslims in the society, non-Muslim communities had vast autonomy to run their own internal religious affairs.

When I lived in Jordan, I heard moving stories about the deep Muslim-Christian ties in the region. Hassan, a Muslim grandfather and shopkeeper I knew in Amman, was originally from Palestine. He and his family had fled their town, northwest of Bethlehem, in 1948 during the wars and fighting that accompanied the creation of the state of Israel. Hassan reminisced to me about his childhood, how he would join his friends at the local church and how his Christian friends would come with him to the mosque. For holidays, their families would bring one another food to celebrate Easter and *Eid al-Fitr*, the Islamic holiday that ends the month of Ramadan. Another of my Jordanian friends, Elhan, a mother of two and a Catholic, recounted a story about when her Muslim neighbors threw a surprise Christmas celebration for her kids. It was shortly after Elhan's mother had died, and, as is custom in many parts of the Mediterranean world, Elhan and her family were not planning to celebrate the holidays that year. Without her knowing, her Muslim neighbors set up a tree in their own home and purchased gifts for Elhan's two young boys. The Muslim family invited up Elhan's family for tea, and surprised them with a Christmas celebration. These beautiful stories of coexistence are ones we in the United States rarely hear in the news.

The stereotype of Muslim intolerance toward those of other faiths results in part from a lack of exposure to these positive stories. It is also a result of the lack of awareness of Western Christians' own history of intolerance, how we have harmed Jews, Muslims, and those of other faiths. During the Crusades, for example, European soldiers massacred Orthodox Christians, Jews, and Muslims in Eastern Europe and the Middle East, in the name of the Catholic Church. During the late fifteenth century, as Christopher Columbus sailed to the Americas, the Spanish Reconquista drove Muslims and Jews out of Spain, or forced them to convert to Christianity. In the United States, Christians—particularly Catholics—cited our faith as a justification for enslaving human beings.[24] We should also recognize that today Christian-majority countries aren't perfect. Our armies and drones have killed thousands of civilians in the Middle East in recent years in the name of "democracy" and "freedom," even while we prop up dictators elsewhere in that region. At home, religious freedom has been a core principle in the United States. But the US government and members of the public have demonized and even discriminated against religious minorities. When mosques are burned down in arson, and people are killed or hurt because of their religion, it is worth asking ourselves if our country truly lives up to its ideal of religious freedom.

Seeing Ourselves—and God—in the "Other"

Stereotypes about Muslims can lead us to believe that Muslims are a uniform and monolithic group. But Muslims are a diverse community numbering around 1.6 billion globally; there are as many Muslims in the world as there are Catholics. Most Muslims don't live in the Middle East or in the Arabic-speaking world—the two countries with the most Muslim residents are Indonesia and Malaysia, which are in Southeast Asia. Muslims live in Africa, Asia, Europe, and the Americas, where they have long contributed to the flourishing of society. In the United States, American Muslims are a small percentage of the population—only about 1 percent. But they live throughout the country and are ethnically diverse—black, South Asian, Arab, Persian, white, and Latino. Some are born overseas, but many are born here. The first Muslims arrived in the Americas from West Africa, forcibly enslaved, long before the founding of the United States.[25]

Stereotypes also imply that Muslims are the "other," a group that is different, foreign, and not like "us." But Muslims share countless commonalities with other religious communities, both on a religious level and also when it comes to our daily lives, concerns, and activities. Polling in the United States shows that Muslims are just as educated as other Americans.[26] Muslims watch college and professional sports, play video games, and recycle just as much as other Americans.[27] Their religion is just as important to them as it is to Christian Americans.[28]

My misconceptions about Muslims—most of which I held on to unconsciously before meeting Muslims—have been dismantled first and foremost through the friendships I've had. This is one of the reasons why interreligious dialogue is so important. When we get to know Muslims as human beings—and not as the caricatures we encounter in the news—our preconceived notions start to fall away. We begin to see God more readily in them, and realize they're much more similar to us than we might have previously thought. The church insists that we don't prejudge Muslims and their faith; we can only form a fair and just opinion of other religions by getting to know their followers.[29] When we begin to acknowledge our stereotypes and implicit biases, and strive to make right our relationships with Muslims, we also improve our relationship with God, who loves us and loves all.

Part II

Encountering God in Islam

3

God Is Greater

No one knows all God's facets.

—Emir Abdelkader (d. 1883), *Spiritual Writings*

My knowledge of Islam has expanded the ways I experience God, think about God, speak about God.

—Fr. Michael Calabria, OFM

As the sun sank down behind the stacks of cement buildings, and the sky turned shades of pink and orange, I hopped into a taxi, feeling very overwhelmed and anxious. It was the end of my first day as a student at the University of Jordan in Amman, and my mind was reeling from the uncertainty that comes with being in an unfamiliar place, far away from family and friends. As I settled into the backseat of the car, the driver changed the radio station, and long, melodic vowels began to emanate from the speakers and fill the cab. It wasn't music, but the Islamic call to prayer.

I quickly realized that it was *maghrib*, sunset—one of the times many Muslims stop their usual activities to pray each day. As the call to prayer, or *adhan*, vibrated throughout the car, it echoed outside throughout the limestone hills of Amman.

A sense of calm came over me as we drove into the increasing darkness. The seat cradled me as the recitation seemed to encourage me to rest and reflect. At the time, my Arabic wasn't good enough to recognize that the *adhan* was indeed telling me to "Come to prayer! Come to well-being!"—*Haiya 'ala as-salah! Haiya 'ala al-falaah!* But I felt peace in that moment, and an assurance that God was with me as I began to navigate my life in Amman.

During my time living in the Jordanian capital, both in college and afterward, the *adhan* became a familiar part of my daily life. Five times a day, the rolling syllables of *Allahu akbar*—Arabic for "God is greater"—could be heard across the city. Chanted from tall minarets and amplified by loudspeakers, the *adhan* reminded Muslims to pray wherever they were—at home, at work, at school, or even at the mall. Sometimes, when I'd visit my local produce shop to buy figs and pomegranates, I'd find the owner praying outside, his rug unrolled on the sidewalk and his body bowing in humble prostration.

I often heard the *adhan* as I threaded my way through the alleyways and side streets of my host family's neighborhood, where the flowers of jasmine trees tumbled over white-painted walls. One of my favorite places to hear the call to prayer was in the hilltop neighborhood of Jabal Amman, from the balcony of a café where I'd often do homework. There I could look over the hills of the city, and see the ruins of the Roman-era citadel and the neon-green lights of distant minarets. As I watched the pigeon keepers release their birds and then call them home, I could feel palpably the sacredness of the place and of the moment.

The *adhan* became something that I, a Catholic, grew to deeply appreciate and enjoy. During my time in Jordan, hearing the Islamic call to prayer would call me to a prayerful state of awareness, and bring me into a disposition of gratitude for the blessings in my life. This practice, from a faith tradition not my own, brought me closer to God.

Encountering God through Islam

This chapter focuses on what my mother once called "the inherent blessings in Islam." Thus far, we've begun to learn about Islam in order to know Muslims better and to grow in relationship with them. These relationships with Muslims—people who are made in God's image—reveal God to us. But, as will be the focus of this chapter, Muslims' *religion* can also help us to grow closer to God.

The idea that we can encounter God through other religions is not just something that I and other Catholics have experienced in our lives. The Catholic Church also teaches it.

The Vatican II document *Nostra Aetate* reads, "The Catholic Church rejects nothing of what is true and holy in these religions. . . . [Their teachings] often reflect a ray of that truth which enlightens all men and women" (2). The church praises what is good and true in other religions, and tells us that the Holy Spirit "blows where it will"—including outside of the church or the Christian community.

When we go into dialogue, we are on the lookout for God and for the good. Father Tom Ryan, a veteran scholar and practitioner of interreligious dialogue, writes that we should enter into dialogue "with a sharp eye and ear for everything that is good, noble, inspiring, and beautiful in their rites and traditions. When we encounter methods of prayer, ethical rules, and spiritual teachings that encourage transcendence of our own selfish inclinations in seeking the good of others, our response is one of appreciation and respect."[1] This approach to other religions requires humility, curiosity, and a willingness to be surprised. We must always keep in mind that "Jesus is radiant and alive in whatever paths lead to God, whatever is true, whatever is life giving," as Jesuit priest and scholar of comparative theology Fr. Francis Clooney puts it.[2] In interreligious dialogue, we are challenged to look for God in unexpected places and even in other religions. Realizing that another religion, like Islam, can help us grow closer to God is something that requires courage and a deep trust in the mystery of God.

Like I did, the Catholic monk Fr. Christian de Chergé felt called to God by the *adhan*. In the 1940s, Fr. Christian spent some of his youth in French-occupied Algeria, where his mother taught him to love his Muslim neighbors and their religious practices. He later spent time there as a soldier in the French army, and eventually became the prior of a Catholic monastery in the Algerian mountains in the 1990s. Islam shaped Fr. de Chergé's Catholic faith life. During Ramadan, Fr. de Chergé fasted as Muslims do, and he developed a habit of taking his shoes off in the chapel, like Muslims do in the mosque. Father de Chergé and his brother monks engaged in interfaith conversation and prayer with the local Muslims in Médéa, the town where they lived. Their monastery, Our Lady of the Atlas, even had a place for Muslim guests to pray when they visited.[3]

In a letter he wrote to his family, which was discovered after he and several of his brother monks were captured and killed during Algeria's civil war, Fr. de Chergé recounted how he often "found that true strand of the Gospel, learnt at my mother's knee, my very first Church, already in Algeria itself, in the respect of believing Muslims."[4]

A scholar of Islam who read the Qur'an in Arabic, Fr. de Chergé saw Islam as a "school" that had something to teach him and his fellow monks.[5] In dialogue, he understood, we acknowledge that we have something to learn about God from Islam. Dialogue is as much about learning and receiving from others as it is about talking and sharing from our own perspective. As individuals, and even as Christian communities, we don't fully grasp the truth of God. Thus, Fr. de Chergé wrote, we must "accept, in the name of Christ, that Islam has something to tell us on behalf of Christ."[6]

In the rest of this chapter, I recount the experiences of Christians whose relationship with God has been shaped by Islam. I will share stories from my own life, and the stories of Catholics and other Christians who have lived among Muslims and learned from their religion. These include saints, priests, popes, religious sisters, and laypeople from both Catholic and Protestant backgrounds, some of whom I have been blessed to know personally. From Islam, each of us has been given an opportunity to encounter God or understand God in new ways.

Look Around, Look Around!

In the Qur'an, nearly four hundred times, God talks about what are called *ayat*. This word refers to the "signs" of God, the miracles in creation that point to God and convey things about the Almighty. The word *ayat* is also used to refer to the verses of the Qur'an itself, which Muslims believe are signs of God, too.

The Qur'an's discussion of God's signs has helped me, a Catholic, to encounter God in creation in a new way. In the Qur'an, God often points to nature to remind humanity of himself: "Do you not see how it is God whom all things praise in the heavens and in the earth, and the birds also on wings of flight? Each truly knows its prayer and its praising and God knows their every deed. For to God belongs the kingdom of the heavens and of the earth. To Him their whole destiny moves" (24:41-42). The rain, wind, cattle, crops, date palms, olives, and even honeybees are just some of God's *ayat* that are mentioned in the Qur'an and upon which humanity is urged to reflect. In all of these things, there are "traces of God's mercy" or *rahma* (30:50).

Human beings—their existence, their abilities, their diversity, and their relationships—are also signs of God, according to the Qur'an. This Qur'anic verse is one of my favorites: "Of His signs is that He created all of you from dust. Behold how you, humanity, are dispersed far and wide. And one of His signs is the fact that He has created partners in marriage to be yours from your own selves, so that, dwelling with them, you might find rest. And He ordained mutual love and mercy between you. Truly in this are signs for those who reflect. The very creation of the heavens and of the earth are signs of His, and the diversity of your languages and color—signs, truly, for all who live" (30:20-22). These portions of the Qur'an have helped me observe God in my own surroundings. I've often thought about these verses while on runs in my neighborhood, when I see bees bumbling among the clover flowers or when I see swallows—which are called "birds of heaven" in Arabic—swooping over the water in the creek.

Constantly, the Qur'an asks its hearers, "Have you not seen . . . ?" (22:18), "Will you not realize . . . ?" (28:72), "Do [people] not reflect . . . ?" (47:24), and "Have they not beheld the heaven above them?" (50:6). God urges, "Oh people! Have ever in mind God's grace toward you" (35:3), so that "perhaps then you might be grateful" (28:73). God's *ayat* are meant to help us remember God, come to know him, and to be grateful to him. When I read these passages in the Qur'an, I think that God must be asking us to develop the attentive and joyful disposition of Eliza Schuyler Hamilton, the historical figure who in Lin-Manuel Miranda's 2015 musical continuously exclaims, "Look around, look around, at how lucky we are to be alive right now!"

Pope Francis seems to appreciate Islam's emphasis on God's signs in creation, too. In his first independently authored encyclical, *Laudato Sì*, he finds inspiration in a sixteenth-century Muslim mystic named Ali al-Khawas. Pope Francis writes, "The universe unfolds in God, who fills it completely. Hence, there is a mystical meaning to be found in a leaf, in a mountain trail, in a dewdrop, in a poor person's face." In the footnote for this passage, the pope writes, "The spiritual writer Ali al-Khawas stresses from his own experience the need not to put too much distance between the creatures of the world and the interior experience of God." The pope goes on to quote the mystic: "There is a subtle mystery in each of the movements and sounds of this world. The initiate will capture what is being said when the wind blows, the trees sway, water flows, flies buzz, doors creak, birds sing, or in the sound of strings or flutes, the sighs of the sick, the groans of the afflicted . . . "[7] Francis cites this Muslim mystic at the beginning of a section in *Laudato Sì* about what the pope calls "sacramental signs." Francis could have chosen something from the two thousand years of Christian mysticism to illustrate the point he wanted to make. But he felt that Ali's perspective—as a Muslim—was the best reference to begin his theological reflections on the sacrament of creation. Francis demonstrates that Islam has something to teach us about how God is revealed in creation. Catholic commentators writing about the encyclical noted that this practice—of citing sources from a non-Catholic faith tradition in a Catholic doctrinal document—is all but unheard of. In citing a Muslim, Pope Francis implicitly acknowledges and affirms the church's teaching that the Holy Spirit does indeed work outside of the church.

The late Kenneth Cragg, a scholar of Islam and an assistant Anglican bishop in Jerusalem in the 1970s (whose translation of the Qur'an I use as the basis for my own in this book), would likely not be surprised by Pope Francis's allusions to Islam in Laudato Sì's section about the "sacrament" of creation. In an essay, Cragg writes, "Islam does not use [the word 'sacramental'], but the theme within it is explicit in the Qur'an's recurrent term *ayah* (pl. *ayat*), seeing nature as a realm of *signs*. . . . Those same *signs* . . . alert us to reverence and thanksgiving."[8]

Thanksgiving is something that Amanda Stueve learned from Islam, too. Now preparing to enter a Dominican religious order in

Kansas, Amanda's spiritual life was ignited when she studied abroad in Morocco during college and again after she graduated. There, as she tells it, she "attended funerals, weddings, naming ceremonies and circumcisions, learned to peel tomatoes, bathed primarily in the public baths during the winter and made homemade Moroccan bread." [9]

Amanda and I met several years later through our Catholic parish when we both lived in Jordan. We often talked about Islam and our own faith while preparing for the confirmation classes we taught to English-speaking high school Catholics. Amanda once recounted to me how she would often complain and whine about little things to her Moroccan host mother. In response, her mother taught her to say *Alhamdulillah*, which means "Praise be to God" or "Hallelujah" in Arabic. The spirituality behind this saying, which Muslims in many parts of the world frequently use, is to be grateful to God always, regardless of one's circumstances. As Amanda described it to me, "Saying *Alhamdulillah* is about being obedient to what God is doing in my life right now." Amanda later realized that this disposition of gratitude is also a huge part of the spiritual life of the Catholic tradition. "If you read the saints," she told me, "that's what they did—they were grateful no matter what." But she first learned this from someone who didn't share her religion.

Called to Prayer

As I tried to fall asleep one night in January 2017, I found my mind racing. It was the day after the Trump administration issued an executive order to ban refugees and those with passports from seven Muslim-majority countries—including those whose homes were in the United States. I was troubled by the order's discriminatory impact on Muslims and couldn't settle down. Wanting to calm my mind and be able to sleep, I whispered to my husband, "I'll be back in a bit"—I felt the need to pray. I grabbed my olive wood rosary and a string of white and blue Islamic *masbaha* beads off my desk and tiptoed into the living room. I quietly turned on a YouTube video of the recitation of *al-asmaa al-husna*, or the "beautiful names" in Arabic, holding my prayer beads. I sat in the dark living room, squinting into the glowing computer screen, and read in Arabic and in English the ninety-nine attributes that Muslims use to speak of God.

Hearing the Islamic litany of God's attributes that night brought me comfort, and helped me channel my mix of emotions. More than once before and since, this practice, called *dhikr* or "remembrance," has brought tears to my eyes. As discussed in chapter 1, the first two names of the Islamic litany connote God's merciful and compassionate nature, God's *rahma*. God's forgiving nature also comes up often in this recitation of God's qualities; two names are variations of the root *gh-f-r*, which signifies forgiveness. *Dhikr*, the Islamic ritual of recalling the divine names, is one I have tried adopting that helps me feel closer to God. Some of the dozens of names are these:

Ar-Rahman	The Entirely Merciful
Ar-Rahim	The Always Merciful
Al-Malik	The King, The Possessor
Al-Quddus	The Holy, The Pure
As-Salaam	The Source of Peace
Al-Khabeer	The Well-Acquainted, or The One Who Knows You Best
Al-Kareem	The Generous
Al-Wadud	The Loving, The Affectionate
Al-Awwal	The First
Al-Akhir	The Last
As-Saboor	The Always Patient and Persistent

Christian historians believe that the recitation of God's beautiful names also impacted the famous St. Francis of Assisi, who had his own personal encounter with Islam during a stay with the Muslim sultan Malik al-Kamil in Egypt in the thirteenth century.[10] Shortly after their encounter during the Crusades, St. Francis wrote a prayer called "The Praises of God," which reads in part:

> *You are holy, Lord, the only God,*
> *   and your deeds are wonderful.*
> *You are strong.*
> *   You are great.*
> *You are the Most High.*

You are almighty.
You, holy Father, are
King of heaven and earth . . .
  You are beauty.
  You are gentleness.
  You are our protector,
  You are our guardian and defender . . .
  Great and wonderful Lord,
  God almighty,
  Merciful Savior.[11]

It's likely not a coincidence that the content and form of St. Francis's prayer sound strikingly similar to the litany of names that Muslims recite. Scholars believe that St. Francis, Catholicism's most famous saint, was deeply shaped spiritually by his exposure to Islam.

Like me, Ray Kim spent the year after he graduated from college in Amman, Jordan. His roommate, Rabieh, was Syrian and Muslim. Rabieh had fled the war in 2012 and was living in Jordan as a refugee. Ray, a Protestant Christian who is now a PhD student studying Islam and Christianity, was struck by Rabieh's practice of praying *salah* five times daily, regardless of what time it was. The five prescribed prayer times for *salah* are not tied to the time on the clock, but are rather determined by the position of the sun in the sky. Consequently, the times for the prayers change slightly each day. In the winter, the *maghrib* sunset prayer could be around 5 p.m., whereas in the summer it would be after 8 p.m.

Ray was in awe of his friend's faithful practice of praying as the times varied so much throughout the course of the year. In an interview for this book, he told me, "Salah is such an inconvenience! That struck me particularly, [having] a level of devotion where you're willing to say: 'Regardless of what I'm up to, I'm willing to drop whatever I'm doing to go fulfill this duty.' And [Muslims' commitment to prayer] is not always just duty-bound. A lot of my friends looked forward to these times of prayer." Ray told me of his difficulty in creating this time in his day to pray as a mainline Protestant in America. And he explained to me how he finds the freedom to schedule his prayer whenever he wants as a cop-out of sorts: "I can say, 'I'll dedicate two hours to God every day to cultivate my devotional practice,' but, in the end, *I* get to *choose* when those two hours are. Those two hours can be at the most convenient times [for me], like right before I go to bed. But praying five times a day when the times change every day—that struck me. . . . [Muslims] really take commitment *and* commandment very seriously. That's one thing that has really stuck with me even until today, and I try to incorporate some of that. The fact that I'm struggling so much with it, reveals to me more just how hard it is."

Like Ray, St. Francis of Assisi was impacted by the prayer practice of the Muslims he met in the Middle East. St. Francis's directives for his fellow friars, which he wrote after his excursion in Egypt, bear striking resemblance to aspects of Islamic practice.[12] For example, St. Francis insisted that Christians be called to prayer publicly by the ringing of a bell or by a herald, much like the *adhan* in Islamic contexts.

Made Better by Islam

As a university professor whose home is decorated with Islamic prayer rugs and icons of Mary and Jesus, Fr. Michael Calabria, OFM, is living out a version of St. Francis's encounter with Muslims in modern times. Father Michael first encountered Islam in Egypt in the 1980s, and is now a Franciscan friar and scholar of the Qur'an who runs St. Bonaventure University's Center for Arab and Islamic Studies. In February 2017, I reached out to interview him over email for this book. In reply, he began by telling me that when he reads the Qur'an, it makes him "want to be a better person," to be the person God has created him to be. He told me about the beauty he finds in the Qur'an's insistence that we be attentive to God's signs, *ayat*, a reaction I share. He also shared a story from his time in Egypt, and how the Islamic concept of *taqwa* has shaped his experience as a believing person:

> I was working at a leprosarium in a village called Abu Za'bal. After leaving the Cairo metro area, our drive took us through a very arid stretch of land—just sandy desert really. One morning, in the distance, I saw a blue road sign. I thought it was directing drivers to another road or some destination. As I got closer I saw

that it said *Udhkur Allah*—"Remember God." That is, in many
ways, what all of Islam says—remember God—to bring God
into your consciousness 24/7. The more we *remember God*, the
more God-centered and truly righteous we become. . . . One
of the most frequently used terms in the Qur'an is the word
taqwa. Many people translate it as "to fear God." But it doesn't
mean to be *afraid* of God; it means rather "to be conscious of
God"—to be aware of God's presence always and everywhere.
To me, that's what all faiths say at their essence. If we truly had
an understanding of God's *omnipresence*, what kind of believers
would we be? As a Catholic Christian, I feel that Jesus' life and
ministry embodied these very concepts, reminding us, highlight-
ing for us—sometimes in powerful and dramatic ways—*God is
with us. Remember . . .*

For Fr. Michael, Islam has become so much a part of his experience—
through his study and teaching—that it is virtually impossible to
separate Islam from the rest of his spiritual life and relationship with
God. He told me, "I find so much of value in the Islamic tradition
that I find it quite difficult now to preach to Catholic congregations
without drawing on something from Islam. I often feel that if I *don't*
bring in something relevant from the Islamic tradition, I'm not telling
'the whole story.'"

Scott Alexander has similarly been impacted by the Islamic tradition. A devout Catholic and the director of the Catholic-Muslim
Studies Program at Catholic Theological Union in Chicago, Scott
has been shaped significantly by the Muslim mystics he studies,
and whose work he reads in their original languages. Scott told me,
"By far, the greatest influences on my spiritual life as a Catholic
have been Muslim. . . . I have spent far more time immersed in
the classics of the great medieval Muslim mystics than in the works
of their illustrious Christian counterparts. . . . Junayd, Hallaj,
Ghazali, Ibn Arabi, Rumi, and many others impact how I think
about and struggle to be faithful to my relationship with God in
Christ." Some of Scott's favorite poetry comes from the mystic and
philosopher Ibn Arabi, who is known as the "Greatest Master" and
who declared, *Al-hubbu deeni wal eemaani!*—"Love is my religion
and my faith!"

During my time conducting research on Muslim-Christian relations in Jordan, I visited Fr. Hanna Kildani, a Catholic priest whose parish was in the outskirts of Amman. On the walls of his office, he had pasted sheets of white printer paper that featured quotes from famous people, including Martin Luther King Jr., Aristotle, and even a character from the film *My Big Fat Greek Wedding*. But the most frequently quoted person on his walls was Ali ibn Abi Talib, an important Muslim leader who was the Prophet Muhammad's cousin and son-in-law. Father Hanna spoke of Ali as a beloved role model who had taught him many lessons.

Father Hanna deciphered and translated for me the intricate Arabic calligraphy of Ali's words printed on the white pages. One phrase talked about rejecting a wealthy lifestyle, and another warned about getting overly attached to worldly relationships. But Fr. Hanna's favorite quote of Ali's was a bit more practical: it was advice on dieting. We walked into the kitchen, where the phrase was pasted above the table and next to a sparkly, woven icon of the Sacred Heart of Jesus, a common devotional image in Catholicism. Ali's quote read, "Whatever you limit yourself to is enough." Fr. Hanna told me that the phrase keeps him from eating too much, and it reminds him of the importance of fasting, a practice that many Catholics have all but abandoned. Standing in the kitchen, Fr. Hanna shared another Arabic saying that demonstrates the way Muslims and Christians are shaped by one another's traditions in the Middle East: "We say that 'the heart of a Muslim is a little bit Christian, and the heart of a Christian is a little bit Muslim.' That's because Muslims receive so much of their religious heritage from Christianity, and because Christians here have been so influenced by Islamic beliefs and culture."

For these diverse Catholics, and for myself, Islam has drawn us closer to God. Its practices, poetry, vocabulary, and—especially—its scripture have impacted us deeply. When I corresponded with Fr. Michael, he articulated what I have often felt, but have had difficulty explaining myself: "[The Qur'an] not only echoes things we find in the Hebrew and Christian scriptures," he told me, "it *magnifies* them. I feel that about Islam: it *magnifies* my faith. It doesn't *replace* my Catholic faith; it underscores and emphasizes aspects of my faith."

Because of Islam, I have found that I see God and his creation in a new way. I think that I know God a bit differently than if I had only encountered God through Christianity. I have found that my Catholicism is complemented, challenged, and bolstered all at the same time, due to my engagement with Islam. The first words of the *adhan*, the call to prayer, are *Allahu akbar*, "God is greater." Hearing these words when I lived in Amman was a constant reminder to me that God always exceeds our expectations and transcends the limited beliefs we have about him.

When I was in high school, and struggling to connect with my Catholic faith, I picked up a secondhand copy of the poetry of the Muslim mystic Rumi. I knew maybe half a dozen Muslims at the time, and barely knew their religion. But the words of Islam's most beloved poet reassured me of the presence of God, at a time when I was unsure of who God was. Rumi helped me to maintain my faith, and to see God in new ways. I found this line in his poetry encouraging and reassuring: "Let yourself be silently drawn by the stronger pull of what you really love."[13] Prompted by Islamic poetry and scripture many times since then, I have lifted my head toward the sky and observed God's grandeur in the blue and yellow buttermilk clouds.

The Prophet Muhammad once said, "Divine breezes from your Lord waft through the days of your life. Listen! Be aware of them."[14] Without Islam, which has been a God-given blessing in my life, I might have missed them.

4

The Width of a Hair

*Seeing things differently does not mean that one is not seeing
the same things. Speaking otherwise of God is not speaking
of another God.*

—Fr. Christian de Chergé, *L'invincible espérance*

*The differences are a less important element than the unity
which, by contrast, is radical, basic, and decisive.*

—Pope St. John Paul II, Speech to the Curia (December 22, 1986)

On a cold night during the spring of my freshman year of college,
I assembled with other Georgetown University students in the
great room of a Christian retreat center in rural Maryland. We all had
come together on the retreat to pray, grow in friendship, and learn
about God. But this retreat was different from others I would attend
later in college—it was grounded in Islamic spirituality.

Wrapping my hair in a white scarf and slipping off my shoes, I
stepped onto a tarp set up in the middle of the room. I squeezed
shoulder-to-shoulder among the other women on the makeshift
prayer rug, facing the direction of the holy city of Mecca as well
as a wall where a large wooden cross was coincidentally mounted.
As the only Catholic student on Georgetown University's Muslim
retreat that winter, I joined in Islam's ritual prayer, *salah*. As the
prayer leader recited the melodic verses of the Qur'an in Arabic, I
followed my friends' movements. For over an hour, we moved from

standing, to bending over, and to prostrating with our foreheads pressed to the floor.

In the years since then, I've prayed *salah* with my Muslim friends many times, usually at the congregational prayer on Georgetown's campus on Fridays. Many of my fellow Catholics, as well as some Muslims, would no doubt take issue with me, a practicing Catholic, praying *salah*. Both communities would likely point to our doctrinal differences around Jesus and the Qur'an, Muhammad, and the Trinity as justification for my nonparticipation. Cognizant of the theological distinctions between the two traditions, I still feel called to pray alongside my Muslim friends as they do. I feel drawn to the ritual even amid my uncertainty and questions over our theological differences.

This chapter is about our theological differences with Muslims, and what we make of them. In my work studying Muslim-Christian relations and researching Catholic perspectives on Islam, I have noticed that we sometimes amplify our apparent differences with Muslims, casting them as a source of conflict or as a cause for nonengagement. This approach focuses on areas of disagreement at the expense of broader similarities. I've also observed that Catholics sometimes assert that we have disagreements with Muslims on certain beliefs about God when in fact we don't. This sometimes occurs due to differences in religious terminology; thus, we miss the similarities at the heart of comparable concepts. This also sometimes happens when our stereotypes, fears, and feelings of superiority get in the way, when we fail to take both an honest and a charitable look at Muslims' religion and the way it is lived out.

In this chapter, I address some of the apparent differences between Christianity and Islam, and identify where we might have more in common than we are often led to believe. I also attempt to clarify some of the differences we do have, which are often misunderstood. In this chapter, I also recount my experience—and that of other Christians—of being positively challenged by Islam's perspective on questions of belief and theology. But first, I tackle one of the questions that comes up often in interreligious dialogue with Muslims: Do we believe in the same God?

"The One and Merciful God"

When I worked as a research fellow at the Bridge Initiative at Georgetown, we conducted a poll of English-speaking Catholics in the United States about their views of Islam. The survey found that 42 percent disagree that Christians and Muslims worship the same God. Only one-third of us agree that we believe in the same God as Muslims.

But recent popes, especially Pope St. John Paul II, have been quite clear about the answer to this question. In a 1985 address to young Muslims in Morocco, he asserted, "We believe in the same God, the one God, the living God, the God who created the world and brings his creatures to their perfection."[1] He reiterated this explicit stance in a public speech in Rome in 1999.

Pope Francis has also implied that Christians, Muslims, and others believe in the same God, like when he said on Holy Thursday in 2016, "All of us together, Muslims, Hindus, Catholics, Copts, Evangelical [Protestant] brothers and sisters—children of the same God—we want to live in peace, integrated."[2]

Lumen Gentium, one of the most important doctrinal constitutions of the Second Vatican Council, speaks of Muslims as "those who acknowledge the Creator," those who believe in the only God that exists, the one whom we as Christians also worship. *Lumen Gentium* then says that Muslims "together with us they adore the one, merciful God" (16), a statement also echoed in the *Catechism of the Catholic Church* (841), the summary of Catholic doctrine. Our popes and the written teachings of the Catholic Church assert that while we might have doctrinal differences with Muslims, we do in fact believe in the same God they do.

If Christians and Muslims didn't worship the same God, then I would not pray *salah* on occasional Fridays with my Muslim friends. Knowing that God draws my Muslim friends to prayer compels me, too. In his encyclical *Redemptoris Missio*, John Paul II asserted that "every authentic prayer is prompted by the Holy Spirit, who is mysteriously present in every human heart."[3] This is a reminder that God is at work in others' religions, especially in their prayer.

For this reason, many Christians feel called to pray with Muslims. Father Christian de Chergé, the Catholic monk in Algeria, had a moving and mysterious experience of interreligious prayer when he was alone in the monastery's church one night. An unnamed Muslim guest arrived, and they prayed together *Surat al-Fatiha*, the *Magnificat*, and the Lord's Prayer. This mystical, three-hour event of interreligious prayer, which Fr. de Chergé insisted was a fact and not a dream, was a central experience in his religious life as a human being and as a Catholic monk.[4]

Praying with Muslims is something that has been formative in the religious life of Fr. Michael Calabria, the Franciscan priest and scholar of Islam at St. Bonaventure University. Long before Fr. Michael was an ordained priest, he learned to pray *salah* as Muslims did and he recounted his experience to me over email (in February 2017):

> In essence, my whole fascination with Islam began with prayer. I remember going to Egypt for the first time in 1981. I was an undergraduate studying Egyptology and was in Egypt to do archaeological work. I knew nothing about Islam at that time. . . . I visited a mosque for the first time, the mosque of Ibn Tulun. I walked into that great, expansive courtyard and was captivated by the simple beauty and tranquility of the space, and its openness to the sky, open to the Creation—and thus, the Creator. . . . Soon after, we began our work in the eastern desert. One morning, just before dawn, I was awakened by the sound of human voices outside my tent. I got up, and in the pink glow of the pre-dawn, I saw some of our workmen praying, prostrating. I was transfixed. It was utterly and serenely beautiful and yet very powerful at the same time. Who wouldn't want to experience that? . . . And so I learned *salah*. *Salah* is fully embodied prayer. Postures signify attentiveness to God, humility before God, repentance and submission to God. I found the postures quite meaningful in my personal prayer. It's particularly profound for me to make *sujuud*—prostrating, touching my forehead to the ground, while praying: "Glory to God, the Most High"—at precisely the moment when I am physically in the lowest position. . . . To some this may sound like syncretism, but I think [St.] Francis would have appreciated the words of the great Sufi, Rabi'a: "In my Soul, there is a temple, a shrine, a mosque, a church that dissolves, that dissolves in God."

The call to pray with Muslims that I and other Christians have heard is rooted in a conviction expressed by the late Jacques Dupuis, a Catholic scholar of interreligious dialogue: "The same God speaks in the hearts of both partners; the same Spirit is at work in both."[5] When we come together to pray with Muslims, we can be confident that the Holy Spirit is present and active, for the Spirit is the source of each person's yearning for God.

Not all Christians will feel comfortable with the idea of praying *salah*. No one should feel compelled to engage in practices that would make a person feel like he or she is compromising on religious beliefs. (Similarly, Christians who *do* wish to pray *salah* should consult their Muslim friends about this decision ahead of time, and get their thoughts.)

Leaving *salah* aside, there are more familiar forms of interreligious prayer that both Muslims and Christians can feel comfortable participating in together. Using a common set of words, Muslims and Christians can invoke God together, asking for his guidance and blessing. Participants should make sure that the words of the prayer don't conflict with the theology of either group. In the appendix I have offered a sample prayer that could be used for joint Muslim-Christian prayer.

Is God "Love"?

One question that often arises in Catholic discussions of Islam concerns love, particularly God's love. Some Catholics have sought to contrast Christianity's motto of "God is love" with what they perceive as a deficit of this idea in Islam. *In Islam*, some Catholics say, *God is only a stern master, not a loving caregiver.* This interpretation satisfies many of our stereotypes, but it isn't consistent with the central tenets of Islam.

For Muslims, God's love is at the center of their religion; they just use a different word for it than we do. As we saw in chapter 1, *rahma* is invoked many times a day by Muslims. In English, it is usually translated as "mercy" or "compassion." But the connotation and centrality of *rahma* in Islam is quite similar to the place of love, or *agape* in Greek, in Christianity. *Agape* is the word in the Christian scriptures, or New Testament, that describes God's self-giving love for humanity. Some Muslim scholars have argued that the best translation for *rahma* would be *agape*.[6] Thus, there is a striking parallel between the line "God is *agape*" in the Bible's First Letter of John, and the idea that God is "ar-Rahman" in the Islamic tradition.

William Chittick, a preeminent Muslim scholar of Sufism, or Islamic mysticism, summarizes the importance of God's love in Islam: "Love is the very Reality of God Himself. It gives rise to the universe and permeates all creation. God singled out human beings for special love by creating them in His own form and bestowing on them the unique capacity to recognize Him in Himself and to love Him for Himself, not for any specific blessing."[7] The whole world is the object of God's loving *rahma*; it encompasses everything.

In the Qur'an and in the Islamic tradition, there are words in addition to *rahma* that speak to God's love for creation and humanity. One of God's ninety-nine names is *al-Wadud*, which is often translated as "the Affectionate," or "the Loving." God is also described as "the Generous," "the Kind," "the Gentle," and "the Friend."[8] Other words for love, like *ishq* and *hubb*, pervade Islamic poetry and mystical writings.

"God Is Always With You"

One of the most apparent creedal differences between Muslims and Christians is about Jesus. For Muslims, Jesus is a highly esteemed prophet and messenger of God. He is referred to as "the Christ," is born of a virgin, and is blessed with the ability to perform miracles. But in Islam, Jesus is not God incarnate in human flesh as he is for Christians. In fact, in Islam no human being is seen as the divine incarnate.

Some Catholics have interpreted this lack of an incarnation in Islam to mean that, to Muslims, God is utterly transcendent—completely outside this world and unknowable to humans. In his book *Crossing the Threshold of Hope*, Pope St. John Paul II says that in Islam God "must remain absolutely transcendent; He must remain pure Majesty." He later goes on: "Some of the most beautiful names in the human language are given to the God of the Koran, but He is ultimately a God outside of the world, a God who is only Majesty, never Emmanuel, God-with-us."[9]

The idea that Islam lacks a concept of divine intimacy is not a reflection of Qur'anic text, the teaching of the Prophet Muhammad, Islamic spiritual writings, and the lived experience of many Muslims. There are passages throughout the Qur'an that speak to God's immanence, or nearness to humanity:

> He knows all that permeates the ground and all that issues from it, what comes down from the heaven and what ascends thither. He is with you wherever you are. God is aware of all you do . . . He knows the innermost heart. (57:4, 6)

> To God belongs the east and the west, and wherever you turn there is the face of God. Truly God is the All-Pervading, All-Knowing. (2:115)

> With truth He created the heavens and the earth. He fashioned you and well He made your frame. To Him is your destiny. His knowledge encompasses everything in the heavens and the earth. He knows your hidden secrets and your manifest deeds. God knows the very heart within. (64:3-4)

> Do not be afraid, you two [speaking to Moses and Aaron]: I am with you: I hear and I see. (20:26)

> We created man: We know the very whisperings within him and We are closer to him than his jugular vein. (50:16)

Omid Safi, a scholar of Islam and the director of the Duke Islamic Studies Center, renders this last Qur'anic verse, in which God refers to himself in the royal "We," this way: "God is closer to you than the beating of your own heart." These verses, which occupy an important place in many Muslims' spirituality, reveal how Islam quite beautifully articulates ideas about God's immanence. Many of God's ninety-nine attributes, like *al-Latif* ("the Kindest One") and *al-Khabeer* ("the Well-Acquainted" or "the One Who Knows You Best"), also connote God's care, attentiveness, and nearness. One of the Prophet Muhammad's famous sayings about God goes like this: "It is said that when you take only one step toward Him, He advances ten steps toward you. But the complete truth is that God is always with you."[10]

Muslims describe beautiful experiences of God's nearness, of feeling personally connected to him through prayer. The Prophet

Muhammad once illustrated the experience of prayer this way: "During prayer, God lifts the veil and opens the gates of the invisible, so that His servant is standing in front of Him. The prayer creates a secret connection between the one praying and the One prayed to. Prayer is a threshold at the entrance to God's reality."[11] This experience is familiar to that of my friend and former colleague Kristin, who converted to Islam from Catholicism during young adulthood. Islam, she felt, gave her a direct, personal relationship to God through prayer, a feeling also attested to by lifelong Muslims. On an interfaith retreat I attended some years back, I heard one Muslim student talk beautifully about how God was her best friend. Many Muslims feel that the absence of Jesus or of priests, who are often viewed as intermediaries, actually allows individuals to have a more direct relationship with their Creator. In Islam, there is no priestly class—every Muslim is his or her own priest.[12]

All of this is not to say that God is never described as transcendent, or unknowable, in the Islamic tradition. God is also understood as beyond our full comprehension. Like in Christianity, descriptions of God's nearness *and* distance are both used, an approach that ultimately reminds believers of the paradox that God is incomprehensible yet still can be known in some ways.

Kneaded like Dough

A significant theological difference between Christians and Muslims revolves around Jesus' role in the two religions. Jesus is a prophet in Muslims' eyes, not a savior or redeemer of humanity. In Islam, there is no original sin, and thus, a savior is not needed to overcome it.

In the summer of 2015, I attended an *iftar*, or Ramadan fast-breaking meal, at the home of a Muslim couple who helped me start to understand the Islamic perspective. They had a new three-month-old baby, and I remarked at how she remained content and cheerful as guests passed her around the room. "It's her *fitra*," Zeyneb, her mother, said.

Fitra, I later learned, is Islam's way of describing the original, primordial state of each human soul. *Fitra* is the soul's predisposition to goodness, to know God and submit to God's will. It is the quality of being in harmony with God and the rest of creation.[13] The three-letter root in Arabic, *f-t-r*, refers to God's creating and originating of the world. It also connotes the act of splitting apart, or of kneading dough. Because God has created humanity, each person has God's imprint on him or her, just as dough or clay would have. As American Muslim writer Davi Barker puts it, *fitra* means having "an active inclination toward the Divine attributes"[14]—goodness, kindness, justice, mercy, and affection. Barker contrasts the Christian notion of original sin with that of *fitra*, which he calls "Original Virtue."

This concept of original virtue has implications for Islamic theology, just as the doctrine of original sin has implications for Christian theology. Because Muslims believe that humanity never completely "fell," humans need God-given guidance—rather than all-out saving—to remain on the path that they are naturally inclined to take. This does not mean that sin isn't real and that repentance isn't necessary—both are central to Islamic belief. But, it does mean that Islam does not require the sort of sacrifice taught by Christianity, in which Jesus atones for the sins of humanity.

This difference is illuminated by the Islamic version of the story of Adam and Eve. According to Islamic tradition, Eve bears no more responsibility for eating the apple and sinning than Adam does. Both the man and woman are equally responsible for their mistake. This version of the Adam and Eve story is different from the one I was introduced to in Catholic school, where Eve, the woman, was portrayed as the initial and primary perpetrator. Additionally, in Islam, Adam and Eve's sin is not passed down to the rest of humanity. Their mistake is not borne by everyone who came after them. Thus, every human being has an inherent *fitra* but is in need of reminders. As Omid Safi explained in an April 2017 email to me for this book, in Islam there isn't original sin but an "original forgetfulness." Consequently, Omid says, there is an "emphasis on *dhikr* and remembrance, to remedy this tendency to forget who and what we are created to be." In the Qur'an, God calls on humanity to notice his many *ayat*, signs, and often refers to his revelation as *huda*, or guidance, for humankind.

As a Christian who was brought up with the idea of original sin, I have grappled with this notion of *fitra*, or original virtue, quite a bit. I believe that we human beings are flawed, but I also believe we are also inherently good so I am very intrigued by the Islamic perspective. Christianity and Islam have different ways of explaining this aspect of the human condition, and I find both ways of seeing it to be illuminating and challenging in a positive way to my faith.

Ray Kim, my Christian friend who lived in Jordan, has also been challenged positively by his engagement with Islamic theology. While reading Islamic mystical (or Sufi) texts during undergrad, he was struck by the concept of *tawheed*, or "divine oneness." Though Christianity and Islam both understand themselves as monotheistic religions, they understand it differently—Christians assert that God is Trinity (Father, Son, and Holy Spirit) while Muslims proclaim God's unity (oneness). For Ray, reflecting on *tawheed* through the texts he encountered in class pushed him to ask deeper, constructive questions about his belief in the Trinity: "Why does the Trinity even matter? What's at stake? Why do we need to get this right?" He doesn't have firm answers to these questions, but has found his relationship with God deepen through pondering them. This is one of the beauties of dialogue: it helps us reflect on our own beliefs about God in a new way, and ask tough questions we never would have asked ourselves otherwise.

Wrestling with theological differences that exist between Christianity and Islam is sometimes difficult. The process is uncomfortable because it doesn't result in hard-and-fast answers. In my own life, pondering Muslims' way of viewing God and the world, and allowing myself to be intrigued by Islam's answers to humanity's theological questions, has been a gift in my spiritual life. I feel better for it—kneaded, like dough. Engaging with the religion of Islam is not something Christians should be afraid of. Rather, we should trust in God, in the Holy Spirit, who animates the world and who, as the Catholic Church says, "blows where it wills."

An Unexpected Answer

In the evening twilight, I rode in a taxi across Jabal al-Weibdeh, a historic neighborhood in central Amman. I was heading to the

Greek Catholic, or Melkite, Church of Saints Peter and Paul, where
I would be attending a special interfaith Holy Week service. As often
happened during my time in Jordan, my cabdriver and I got into a
conversation about Islam and Christianity. This driver was particularly enthusiastic and curious about my focus on interreligious dialogue. He asked in Arabic, "So what is the main, central difference
between Christianity and Islam?"

From his tone, I could tell that his inquiry might be a trick question. In my head, I wondered in English how to respond: *What answer does he have in mind? What point is he trying to make by asking
me this? Should I talk about the disagreement over Jesus' divinity,
Islam's denial of the Trinity, or Christianity's rejection of Muhammad's prophethood?* I decided to go for the first point, because it
seemed the easiest to explain in Arabic and is also a difference that
relates to other theological disagreements.

"Christians believe Jesus is God and Muslims don't," I said in
Arabic. The driver seemed unsatisfied with my answer. He didn't
deny that this doctrinal difference existed but immediately jumped
to qualify it. "Take a piece of your hair. One piece. The strand is so
thin, you can barely grasp it. This strand of hair is what divides us,"
he said, demonstrating with his hands above the steering wheel. His
metaphor reminded me of a story from early Islamic history, when
the new Muslim community traveled to Christian-ruled Ethiopia.
Having been persecuted in Mecca, Muhammad's followers sought
protection under the king, Negus. But the Christian king's advisors
were preoccupied with the religious differences between themselves
and the refugee Muslims, asking the visitors what they believed
about Jesus. The king walked up to Jaafar, the leader of the Muslim
delegation, and with his staff drew a line in the sand. "The difference
between us and you," he said, "is no thicker than this line."[15] He then
welcomed them and assured his Muslim guests of his protection.

The gesture of my Muslim cabdriver, like the story of the Christian king, helped remind me that our theological differences are thin,
almost invisible. Yet, sometimes, we allow the strands of doctrinal
difference to loom too large, to become impassable barriers between
us. We forget about our shared values, our shared humanity, and our
need for solidarity. However, if we redirect our focus from the single

strands, step back, and admire the full head of hair on the other, we may find in ourselves the ability to befriend and even bless the other.

Which is what my cabdriver did as he dropped me off outside the church.

"*Allah ma'ik,*" he said, "God be with you."

Part III

Reembracing God
in Christianity

5

Arriving Where We Started

We shall not cease from exploration,
And the end of all our exploring
Will be to arrive where we started
And know the place for the first time.

—T. S. Eliot, "Little Gidding V," *Four Quartets*

Every night during my senior year at Georgetown, I attended Mass in a small crypt chapel on Georgetown's campus. A little before ten o'clock, I'd put away my homework, close up my laptop, and walk across campus to the sanctuary. The crypt chapel was an intimate space with dark stone walls and low arched ceilings. Orthodox-style icons flanked the altar and colorful lanterns suspended above reflected dim light onto the silk threads of the white altar cloth. That chapel was my spiritual home that year, a place I'd go to pray surrounded by dozens of students who became close friends. The serenity of the space, the thoughtful homilies from the Jesuit priests, and the mystery of the Mass nurtured my relationship with Jesus.

My practice of Catholicism wasn't always that regular, or devoted. When I arrived at Georgetown a few years prior, after having gone to Catholic schools and being surrounded by fellow Catholics for my whole life, I wasn't sure I wanted to be Catholic anymore. It wasn't until my engagement with Muslims and their religion that I eventually made the conscious effort to reembrace the faith of my childhood.

In this chapter, I reflect on how interreligious dialogue with Muslims can help us connect to God through our own Christian tradition. I will trace my own experience, how I came back to Catholicism in response to the beauty I saw in Islam, and out of a curiosity sparked by my dialogue with Muslims. I will also share the stories of others whose Christianity has been impacted by their exposure to Islam. In this chapter, I'll also tackle a question that often arises out of interfaith dialogue, a question that I continue to ponder: Can Muslims go to heaven?

Curiosity and Questions

Some of my earliest memories are of being in church. I remember sitting on the pew at our church in Indianapolis, drawing pictures of a skinny-limbed Jesus while nibbling on Cheerios. When it was time to sing a song, I would climb up on the kneeler, open the green *Gather* book, place it on the back of the next pew, and sing along to words that I couldn't read but knew from memory. During the eucharistic prayer, I recited the words in my head as the priest did aloud. At the end of Mass, I'd often run out to the garden where a white statue of Mary was situated. Her arms were open wide, gesturing downward toward the pebbles and flowers around her. I don't know why I felt drawn to her, but my parents tell me that I greeted her every Sunday after Mass.

As a child, I had a curiosity for religion and sought out moments for connection with God, even if not in a conscious way. I was an altar server at Mass and, as I got older, worked behind the scenes to coordinate the school Masses. I felt a sense of reverence each time I approached the tabernacle to count how many Hosts were already consecrated and estimate how many the priest would need for the next Mass. I loved going to church on occasional Sundays at a local Carmelite monastery. The sisters, who lived a semi-cloistered lifestyle in the castle-like monastery, inspired me by their prayerfulness, but also by the way they voraciously read the news. Even as the sisters were largely removed from the day-to-day activities of the outside world, I saw that, through prayer, they were intimately connected to the joys and sufferings of people near and far.

As I grew older, though, my Catholic community began to feel insular, and the way Catholicism was practiced felt formulaic. My community was primarily made up of Catholics; I went to Catholic parochial grade school, and the majority of my extended family was Catholic. I was curious to learn about ways of living and believing outside of my own community, and, though my parents encouraged exploration, my broader Catholic community didn't. I could recite all the typical prayers, and knew the names of all the items used during the Mass, but I wasn't emotionally or intellectually stimulated by the way Catholicism was observed at my parish and school. I understood that we believed Jesus was divine, and that he saved humanity by his death and resurrection, but I didn't know *why*, or what that really meant. My curiosity about God and religion was often left unsatisfied by my Catholic school religion classes because no one ever provided me real answers as to why these beliefs were meaningful or important.

When I started attending Indianapolis's Jesuit-run high school, I found my horizons broadened and my curiosity engaged. Bored by my own faith, I welcomed the opportunity to learn about other religions in the freshman World Religions course. I got a copy of the *Bhagavad Gita*, a Hindu scriptural text, and a book of the poetry of Rumi, the famous thirteenth-century Muslim mystic. These texts, and my initial exploration of other religions during high school, helped me connect with God and satisfied some of the spiritual hunger I was feeling. I was also excited by the social justice work of some Catholics I knew, but became frustrated that most Catholics in my community seemed to be close-minded toward others or skeptical of activism.

I never stopped going to church, but it often wasn't intellectually or emotionally engaging for me. When I recited the Nicene Creed, the words felt hollow. I felt I couldn't really assent to what the congregation was saying, and found myself assigning broad symbolic meaning to doctrines that, to me, seemed to lack consequence. As I prepared to start college at Georgetown, also a Catholic and Jesuit school, I wondered if another religion like Islam might provide me with the connection to God that I sought. One summer night, I tried prostrating on my bed as one does in Muslim prayer. I thought Islam might provide me with the depth of faith that I was missing in Catholicism.

Theology Over Chai

It wasn't until college that I began to develop deep friendships with students and chaplains who were Muslim. In high school I knew a few Muslims, like Nadir, who I spoke of previously in chapter 1. But, other than him, I didn't know well anyone who was Muslim. But during my first months at Georgetown, I met Wardah, a girl who lived in my dorm. She and I became fast friends, bonding over funny YouTube videos during study breaks in our dorm. Since we were also both interested in religion, Wardah and I, along with another friend, Joanna, started an informal interfaith dialogue group. We met in one of our dorm rooms and brought along our holy books. Joanna, who was Protestant at the time, but has since converted to Catholicism, brought her Bible, and Wardah brought the Qur'an. For our first meeting, I brought books that at the time held spiritual significance for me: *The Alchemist* by Paulo Coelho, the *Bhagavad Gita*, and a Jesuit prayer book. Each week, we planned a topic to discuss, but more often than not we veered into unplanned yet fascinating conversations. Sipping hot chocolate and tea, we talked about the nature of God, traditions, rituals and holidays, and similarities and differences between biblical and Qur'anic stories. I remember how excited we became when we realized the words of a story about Abraham in the Bible and the Qur'an matched up almost perfectly.

Inevitably during our conversations, questions about Christian belief arose that I had never considered before. Sometimes I was able to use formulaic Catholic language to respond, but neither I nor my friends could understand the significance behind the jargon. Often, I had no idea how to answer their queries. My lack of knowledge of my own faith quickly became apparent to me. *What is the significance of believing in Jesus? Why is the Trinity important?* I realized that my Catholic education up until that point had given me the *what* of the faith, but not the *why*. I was already carrying deep theological questions, and our weekly interfaith dialogues caused new ones to arise. I wanted to learn more.

To delve into my own faith tradition more, I signed up for a class at Georgetown called Introduction to Biblical Literature. The course, taught by Paul Heck, a Catholic professor who is an expert in both

Christianity and Islam, helped me to better understand the Bible and also the rituals of the Mass. Subsequently, when I went to Mass, I felt more engaged and emotionally connected, and the boredom I had felt in high school started to dissipate. It wasn't the Mass that had changed—the readings and rituals were the same—but my own understanding of what they meant was enhanced. Thanks to what I learned in class, I was able to better comprehend what God was trying to tell me through scripture, and to feel a powerful sense of God's presence during the Eucharist. Throughout the rest of college, I took numerous courses in Christian theology, and found my relationship with Jesus grow as I read the mystical texts of St. Teresa of Ávila and Julian of Norwich.

Falling Back in Love

Early on at Georgetown, I also started going to events hosted by the Muslim Student Association, and eventually joined the group's governing board. I attended frequent meetings and numerous *iftars*, the fast-breaking meals during the Islamic holy month of Ramadan. Wardah also invited me and two other friends to live together in the campus's Muslim living-learning community. The group of dorm rooms fostered community among Muslim students and others who wanted to connect over faith and socialize outside of the typical party scene. During my time with the Muslim student community, I was struck by the sense of community they had. They supported one another in their spiritual lives and in their practices like fasting. In my own Catholic context, I never really had a religious community of peers. I had often felt like a loner in my faith tradition.

I was also struck by my friends' commitment to prayer. When we roomed together, Wardah woke up early in the morning to pray *salah*. Sometimes, when we'd be working on homework, she would stop in the middle of assignments to pull out her prayer rug. I admired Wardah's consistency in prayer, because at the time, I lacked any sort of commitment in my relationship with God, other than going to Mass on Sundays. Wardah and other friends who made time for *salah* told me how it helped them step away from the stresses of school and refocus on what was most important: God. I wanted that kind of a prayer life, too.

Noticing the strong faith community that my Muslim friends had, and witnessing their dedication to prayer, I felt compelled to engage these aspects of my own faith tradition. With the intent of improving my daily prayer habits, I signed up for Catholic retreats offered for students. Forms of prayer like the Daily Examen, devised by the founder of the Jesuit order of priests, St. Ignatius of Loyola, helped me to notice God more in my daily life. I developed a deep, personal friendship with Jesus, who became a companion to me on campus and as I eventually explored the Middle East. I also joined a small Catholic Bible group that provided me with a community with whom I could reflect on scripture. By the end of college, I was attending Mass five or six times a week, finding it a comforting part of my day where I could reflect in gratitude. Through my Catholic faith community, I made new friendships, deepened old ones, and even met the person who would later become my husband.

I grew to love my Catholic faith again. I consciously chose Catholicism for the first time, and felt like I should have received the sacrament of confirmation then, rather than back in high school. My reembracing of Catholicism would not have been possible without my exposure to Islam and my immersion in the Muslim community.

On an emotional level, I was compelled by the emphasis on prayer and the sense of spiritual community I witnessed among my Muslim friends to seek out those things in my own tradition. Intellectually, Islam offered me a critical distance from which to view the faith of my childhood. It gave me a reference point from which I could more clearly see my own tradition, which, for much of my life, had been too close and too familiar for me to see its beauty or to really grapple with its theology. Dialogue with Muslims raised questions and presented alternative viewpoints that allowed me to reflect back on Catholicism with a new perspective and a curiosity to learn more.

When I went on the Muslim Students Association retreat in college, we spent much of the first night praying *salah*. As the prayer leader recited the long *ayat* in Arabic, I began to feel distracted. My body was not used to the movements, and I couldn't understand most of the words. Throughout the standing portions of prayer, when Muslims fold their arms over their rib cage, I had a desire to fold my hands, interlacing my fingers as I was used to, praying before bed or in church. I eventually did fold my hands, and, thanks to that familiar position of prayer from my Christian tradition, I found my mind focusing on God more easily. Islam, a faith not my own, became the medium through which I came to love the faith of my childhood.

Some of my fellow Catholics discourage interfaith dialogue when a person is in a state of uncertainty about one's Christian faith. They are concerned that if young Catholics are not very informed about and secure in their faith, being exposed to other religions will get them off-track and perhaps draw them away from the religion. But my experience, and that of other Catholics who have found their Christian faith positively impacted by engagement with Islam, demonstrates that interfaith exploration can result in a deepening of one's Christian faith and practice. Pope St. John Paul II also assures us in his encyclical *Redemptor Hominis* that participation in dialogue "does not at all mean losing certitude about one's own faith or weakening the principles of morality."[1] Rather, he says elsewhere, "the 'beliefs and the moral values of the followers of other religions can and should challenge Christians to respond more fully and generously to the demands of their own Christian faith.'"[2]

Holy Envy

Krister Stendahl, a Lutheran bishop and a professor who is now deceased, was well known for his work on interreligious dialogue. He coined the term "holy envy" to describe his feeling of admiration, and even desire, for aspects of other faith traditions. Many Catholics and other Christians I know have described to me a similar experience they've had in dialogue with Muslims. Scott Alexander, the Catholic professor of Islam I mentioned in chapter 3, told me that his love of the Liturgy of the Hours—the daily prayer schedule of the Catholic Church—was the result of the holy envy he had after witnessing the dedication to prayer that his Muslim friends had. He shared this with me in an email (in February 2017):

> When I was young and first studying Islam as an undergraduate, I had just discerned not to pursue a vocation to the priesthood. At the same time, I was determined to continue seeking a deeper connection with God, and found the fact that all Muslims

were enjoined to offer ritual worship at least five times daily deeply compelling. . . . I wanted what Muslims had and came to realize that, following the stunning example of my Muslim sisters and brothers, I could incorporate the Divine Office into my life as a layman.

Scott explained that he's not always as regular with his prayer as he'd like to be, but that "whatever dedication to prayer I do have . . . has been gifted to me by Muslims."

Amanda, my friend who is entering the order of religious sisters in Kansas, had a similar experience during her time in Morocco. She told me that living with Muslims changed her prayer life. "You see that life there really has its own rhythm of returning to God constantly." Wanting that rhythm, and the sense of calm that comes with it, she started praying the Liturgy of the Hours herself. Now, several years later, she is becoming a religious sister.

Many Catholics I know strongly admire Muslims' practice of fasting. During Ramadan, a month on the lunar Islamic calendar, able-bodied Muslims fast each day from food and water from dawn to sunset, a practice intended to deepen one's connection to God and engender compassion for the poor. In the evening, the fast is often broken with water and dried date fruits—and a big meal with family and friends. The month of Ramadan commemorates the first revelation of the Qur'an to Muhammad. According to Islamic tradition, Muhammad was praying in a cave when, through the angel Gabriel, God bestowed on him this message:

> Recite, in the name of your Lord, who created
> Created man from a sperm-cell.
> Recite, how your Lord is the Most Generous
> Who taught by the pen,
> Taught man that which he knows not. (96:1-5)

During Ramadan, Muslims schedule additional prayers into their day, and many endeavor to read the entire Qur'an throughout the thirty days. Diverting one's attention from more bodily concerns, like food, is intended to direct one's mind more to God and to those less fortunate. Many Catholics see the positive spiritual effects that fasting has on their Muslim friends. Also aware that fasting has been an important part of Christian life since the earliest days, these Christians attempt to emulate Muslims' commitment. Michael Bayer, who works as the senior director for youth and young adults in the Diocese of Raleigh, told me he sees something "transformative" about the Ramadan fast, and it inspires him to be a "less complacent fast-er" during the Christian season of Lent. Over the last several years, I have only done the Ramadan fast for a total of half-a-dozen days. It was a challenging, but rewarding, experience, and my Muslim friends tell me it becomes easier when one truly directs the hunger toward God and develops real dependence on him.

The *iftar* celebrations each night during Ramadan were where I first remember having this feeling of holy envy, a longing for the sense of community and dedication to prayer that my Muslim friends had. Seeing the Georgetown Muslim community come together to pray and eat each night, my reaction was, "Hey, I want that, too!"

Who Is Saved? And How?

Sitting in the backseat of our minivan on the way to St. Matthew School in fourth grade, I posed a question to my mom about Jesus, heaven, and salvation. Aware that there were many, many people in the world who didn't believe in Jesus, I asked, "Do you think God would exclude people who aren't Christian from heaven just because they don't believe in Jesus? I think God is nicer than that."

At the time, I didn't know anyone who was Muslim, or Jewish, or Hindu. Despite this, the idea that those following other religions were assured condemnation after death didn't sit well with me. My discomfort with this notion persisted as I grew up, got to know Muslims, and began to reclaim Catholicism more consciously in college. But I was hesitant to return wholeheartedly to a faith that, I assumed, firmly closed the door of salvation to non-Christians (a stance I thought Catholicism must certainly support). It wasn't until I encountered the documents of the Second Vatican Council that I found my concerns addressed. While the holy envy I felt for aspects of Islam helped me reembrace my Catholicism, I am not sure I could have remained within the fold of the Catholic Church if I had never encountered the church teaching on other religions formulated during Vatican II.

In a class on Catholicism at Georgetown, I read numerous documents issued during the Vatican II conference in the 1960s, many of which—I was surprised to find—spoke about the church's view of those of other faiths. Reading *Lumen Gentium*, the council's Dogmatic Constitution on the Church, I learned that my assumptions had been wrong, and found that the church leaves the door of salvation poetically ajar for those of other faiths. Echoing St. Paul, the document reminds the reader that "the Savior wills that all men be saved." After speaking about Jews, *Lumen Gentium* says, "But the plan of salvation also includes those who acknowledge the Creator, first among whom are the [Muslims]: they profess to hold the faith of Abraham, and together with us adore the one, merciful God, who will judge humanity on the last day." *Lumen Gentium* goes on to say the plan of salvation also includes those who sincerely seek God and live by their conscience, and even those who "have not yet arrived at an explicit knowledge of God" (16).

These statements pleasantly surprised me when I first encountered them, not expecting that this would be the Catholic Church's stance. These teachings gave me consolation to know that in the church's eyes my Muslim friends weren't *a priori* excluded from salvation. The many Muslims I know are the same as my fellow Catholics—human beings who strive to follow God, and live a good, happy life of service to others. Many of them, including close friends who have taught me much about God, exemplify extraordinary generosity, kindness, and self-sacrifice. I could not accept a faith tradition that automatically excluded them from the hope of heaven.

The "communion of saints" is a term the Catholic Church often uses to talk about those who are in heaven, who are saved—that is, unified with the Body of Christ. Father Christian de Chergé, the monk who lived and died in Algeria, wrote about the communion of saints as a reality "where Christians and Muslims, and so many others along with them, share the same joy of sons and daughters."[3] Years before his own death, de Chergé's friend, Mohamed, had been killed for protecting Christian. Father de Chergé was convinced that Mohamed, who had sacrificed himself to save him, would achieve salvation: "For I know that I am able to place firmly at this destination of my hope at least one Muslim, that beloved brother, who lived up to the moment of his death the imitation of Jesus Christ."[4] In Fr. Christian's "last testament," a letter he wrote to his family and friends before he died, he wrote about his hope for heaven:

> [M]y most avid curiosity will be set free.
> This is what I shall be able to do, God willing:
> immerse my gaze in that of the Father
> to contemplate with him His children of Islam
> just as He sees them, all shining with the glory of Christ,
> the fruit of His Passion, filled with the Gift of the Spirit
> whose secret joy will always be to establish communion
> and restore the likeness, playing with the differences.[5]

My hope and curiosity is similar to that of Fr. Christian. To my mind, the communion of saints must be full of Muslims.

So how does this work? How might Muslims be saved? Writings by Fr. Daniel Madigan, a Jesuit priest and scholar of Islam who teaches at Georgetown, provide a helpful Catholic framework for beginning to ponder this. In an article about *Nostra Aetate*, the Vatican II document that focuses on other religions, Madigan writes that "in the Christian understanding, being saved means being incorporated into the divine life through the person of the fully divine, fully human one"—Jesus.[6] This incorporation into the Body of Christ, he explains in another essay, is achieved when people live out Jesus' self-sacrificing love. This self-emptying love can be lived out by anyone, not just people who claim the Christian religion. Thus, Madigan describes his hope for Muslim friends' salvation: "On the way I have encountered others who know and live the truth of self-emptying love, even if they have not recognized it in the Cross of Christ. I trust that, as St. John tells us, all of us who are living in love are living, and will live forever, in God."[7]

Grateful for the Gift

My process of reclaiming Catholicism after encountering Islam occurred differently than many people might expect. Some may assume that I simply didn't like Islam's beliefs and practices, and thus I ran for the hills—back to Catholicism. But I found so much beauty in Islam, so many things I love, and this journey helped me to find beauty in Catholicism, too.

In the years since I consciously reembraced Catholicism, I've been asked if I am Muslim or if I'm converting to Islam. It shouldn't be a surprise to me that people have asked these questions, given my involvement with the Muslim community, my work researching Islamophobia, the fact that I pray *salah* sometimes, and that I can recite bits of the Qur'an in Arabic. But the first time someone posed the question, I was amused, because it was during a time in college when I felt more Catholic than I ever had previously. Even as I am a practicing Catholic, Islam has remained a central part of my life. My engagement with Islam doesn't take away from my practice of Catholicism but rather enhances it. As I experienced on the prayer rug on the Muslim retreat years ago, Islam continues to remind me of what is familiar and comforting about Christianity, while also making it feel brand new.

Father de Chergé wrote about Islam as a gift not just given to his Muslim friends, but also one gifted by God to him: "The faith of the other is a gift from God, albeit a mysterious one. Therefore it commands respect. . . . And this gift given to the other is also intended for me, to urge me in the direction of what I have to profess." [8]

Islam has helped me respond to God's call in my life. It has helped me be more attentive to the way God operates in the wider world and in the lives of my Muslim friends, but also how God is present in the faith tradition I grew up in. Islam makes me a better Catholic.

6

The Dialogue of Life

Christians can affirm that they need Muslims
in order to live out their own faith.

—Fr. Christian Salenson, *Christian de Chergé: A Theology of Hope*

One night during Mass in the crypt chapel at Georgetown, I heard a muddled yet melodic sound coming from the next room. Reverberating faintly through the wall behind the tabernacle, the focal point of the chapel, the sound resembled the intonation I was so used to hearing during the call to prayer in Jordan. I slowly realized that on the other side of that wall was the *musallah*, the Muslim prayer room, and that what I was hearing was recitation of the Qur'an. At the same time that many Catholic students had gathered for Mass in the crypt chapel, many Muslim students were assembled for the nighttime *isha* prayer next door. This simultaneous worship would happen every night during my senior year, and I could occasionally hear the sound of the Arabic prayers through the *musallah* and chapel's shared wall.

That year, record numbers of Catholic and Muslim students started attending their respective services at 10 p.m. Catholic students were forging deeper faith commitments, just as Muslim students were. I don't think this confluence was mere coincidence. In choosing to worship God in between homework assignments each night, we were—even if indirectly—witnessing to one another and to others the importance of making time for God. In my experience, the impact was more direct: if it hadn't been for the group of believers on the other side of the chapel wall, I wouldn't have started attending nightly Mass in the first place.

My deepened connection to Catholicism didn't end my participation with the Muslim community or my engagement with Islam. As an undergraduate, I worked with both the Muslim and Catholic student groups to facilitate interfaith dialogues like the one I had with Wardah in our dorm room. Today, I continue to occasionally attend *salah* on Fridays, and my friendships with Muslims—as well as my study of Islam in my doctoral program—continue to shape my understanding of God. I often find myself invoking God through the Arabic version of "hallelujah"—*Alhamdulillah*—or the following prayer, which Moses prays in the Qur'an:

> Oh Lord, open my heart,
> Make my task easy for me,
> Undo the knot of my tongue
> So that they may understand what I have to say. (20:25-28)

In my life as a practicing Catholic, my Muslim friends and Islam are there with me. They are an inseparable part of my life and play an important role in my relationship with God.

Our journey of dialogue with Muslims is not a one-time endeavor, but rather an ongoing way of living. For the Catholic Church, the "dialogue of life" is the form of dialogue that goes beyond an activity scheduled on the calendar. It happens in our daily lives when we encounter people of other faiths with a disposition that, as Pope Francis puts it, "offers human warmth" to others. Living dialogue in our daily life is, according to the Catholic Church, part of our "Christian vocation."[1]

Dialogue helps us live out our Christian faith better by helping us to continually deepen our relationship with God. It also prompts us to reexamine the way we live out our religion, and reminds us of the demands of our Christian faith: to love our neighbors better. In this final chapter, I discuss the rewards, challenges, and responsibilities of living as Christians in dialogue with Muslims.

As we've already seen, dialogue brings meaningful moments of connection. It results in a kind of "spiritual solidarity" of believers across religious lines, something I'll elaborate on in this chapter by recounting the joys I and others have experienced through dialogue. Despite these rewards, dialogue doesn't come without its difficulties. Often, we face opposition from within our own Christian communities, which, as we saw briefly in chapter 2, sometimes fall into un-Christian ways of treating our Muslim brothers and sisters. In this chapter, I share from my own experience about these challenges. Lastly, I talk about the responsibilities that come along with a life of dialogue. Our relationships with Muslims, as well as our own Christian religion, require us to support our Muslim friends' spiritual lives and to work to make our own Christian communities better expressions of God's love. Being in dialogue with Muslims leaves us no choice but to live out our Christianity differently.

The Reward: Sharing Prayers

One evening in college, I received a text message from Wardah. We were about to meet at the dining hall, which was adjacent to my dorm. "Hey can I come up and pray in your room before we go to eat?" she asked. There wasn't time to head over to the *musallah*, her own dorm, or another quiet place before we were supposed to meet up with friends at the dining hall, and she wanted to complete the sunset, or *maghrib*, prayer. "Absolutely," I replied. Wardah and I had been roommates the year prior in the Muslim living-learning community, and she had prayed in our shared space often. It was her regular prayer habits that had initially compelled me to register for Catholic prayer retreats. When Wardah arrived and began her prayer, it gave me the opportunity to pause my day and pray. Sitting on my bed, I pulled out my Jesuit prayer book for a few quiet moments before we went down to the dining hall.

In this moment, Wardah and I were able to support one another in our respective relationships with God. We helped one another respond to God's call—I provided a place to pray, and her prayer in turn prompted mine. The beautiful thing about dialogue, the Catholic Church says, is that we, together with Muslims, "are invited to deepen [our] religious commitment."[2] If Wardah had decided not to pray the *maghrib* prayer that night, I would not have gotten up from my computer to sit in prayer. God called me through her, through her Islam, and through our friendship. For me, one of the richest rewards of interreligious dialogue with Muslims is that when my friends are called to pray, I am, too.

Muslims are an important part of my faith community today. On Christmas every year, I receive numerous text messages and Snapchat videos from Muslim friends around the world wishing me a "Merry Christmas!" I often feel more comfortable talking about religion with my Muslim friends than I do with fellow Catholics. When I worked at the Bridge Initiative, I had illuminating and enriching conversations with my Muslim colleagues, Nazir, Kristin, and Mobashra, about God and our personal spiritual lives. Amanda Stueve feels similarly comfortable talking about religion with Muslim friends. She told me that for her, a devout Muslim often makes a better confidant when she wants to talk about her faith than someone who might have grown up Catholic but no longer practices the faith. She explained that Muslims share with Catholics the foundational, basic parts of the spiritual life, things like a constant returning to God through prayer, and an emphasis on trust in God.

Another moving aspect of forming religious bonds with Muslims is the act of praying *for* one another. Muslim friends have asked me to pray for small things like their success in exams, and for big things like success in their marriage. Knowing they pray for me, too, is incredibly meaningful. They have faith in my relationship with God, and I have confidence in theirs. When I know of a person or situation that needs prayers, I will often ask my Muslim friends to make *dua*, a petition prayer. My Muslim friends and I trust that one another's prayers will reach our common Creator. As Fr. Fadi Daou, a Maronite Catholic priest and the head of an interfaith organization in Lebanon called Adyan, said in a 2016 interview with *National Catholic Reporter*, "We are talking about . . . recognizing, in Christian terms, that the Holy Spirit is working in the spiritual experience of others."[3]

These rewards of dialogue emerge out of what Nayla Tabbara, a Muslim theologian who works with Fr. Fadi at Adyan, calls "spiritual solidarity." This expression was coined by the Catholic leaders in the Middle East in a 1994 statement titled Called Together in Front of God. In the interview with *National Catholic Reporter*, Tabbara said spiritual solidarity is about giving over a space within one's self "where the other dwells" so that the other becomes "a part of me."[4] She believes that, through real, interfaith encounters, we no longer think of the other as outside our own community.

This kind of solidarity can be expressed in subtle yet beautiful ways between people who hardly know each other. At my wedding reception, my dad met Nazir, my good friend from the Bridge Initiative. As they were sharing stories about their children, Nazir stopped and pulled his prayer beads out of his pocket. Nazir explained that he wanted my dad to have his *masbaha*—the prayer beads from Jordan he always carries with him—which had been a source of peace and comfort for him for a long time. Moved by such a profoundly kind gesture, my dad now carries those beads in his pocket every day, aware of the spiritual significance they held for Nazir. My father says that they symbolize a bond the two of them forged that day, a connection between them in their experiences of fatherhood, and serve as a reminder that people of very different backgrounds, generations—and even faiths—can have so much in common.

The Challenges: Chain Emails and Tough Conversations

One afternoon when I was in high school, I opened my inbox to find a chain email from a family friend from my parish. The message sought to cast suspicion on all Muslims because of the violence committed by a few, and said that the majority of Muslims were "irrelevant" and even "our enemy." The anonymous author asked readers to forward the message to family and friends, and I saw that the email had already circulated among prominent members of my Catholic parish community.

I didn't know many Muslims at the time, but the message left me shaking and speechless. I was upset and confused that a family friend, someone from my own Catholic community, could espouse or promote these ideas, effectively lumping terrorists together with my friend from high school, Nadir. The woman who forwarded the message was the mother of a close friend of mine, whose house I had gone to for countless sleepovers and birthday parties. I knew this woman was by no means a hateful person, and that she and the many in my parish who had sent the email were not trying to hurt anyone by sending it. Still, it was difficult to understand why and how they would do this.

One of the most difficult things for me about reembracing Catholicism was knowing of the prejudice toward Muslims that exists in my own faith community. Since receiving the chain email back in high school, I've seen fear and ignorance concerning Muslims bubble up in subtle ways in conversations with fellow Christians. I've also heard stories from my Muslim friends about episodes of misunderstanding and mistreatment they've experienced at the hands of those who share my faith. On account of my work researching and writing about Islamophobia, I also have received swathes of nasty messages from Christians on social media. Employing stereotypes and hateful tropes about Muslims, anonymous Christians online have said that I must enjoy being treated like a second-class citizen by Muslims or even being sexually assaulted by them. People have said that I have "the blood of Middle Eastern Christians on my hands" and that I should be harmed. Frightening tweets and Facebook messages from those with anti-Muslim agendas have even targeted my husband and my mom.

But the most hurtful message on social media from a fellow Christian was one I didn't see until five years after it was initially posted. It was shared by a young woman with whom I had gone to school and played Catholic youth sports. While perusing Twitter, I came across a tweet in which she referenced my personal website—and my supposed "besty": "Osama bin Laden." Looking at the date on the tweet, I realized that she posted this tweet just days after I had published a blog post titled "My Best Friend is Muslim," which featured pictures of Wardah and me. In her tweet, this young woman wasn't just making a vague, stereotypical comment about Muslims (something that would be problematic enough). She was directing her insult at a specific living, breathing person—Wardah. In her mind, my friend was no different than a terrorist mastermind. As with the chain email sent by the family friend, this tweet was shared with others in our Catholic community; she tagged a number of girls with whom we had gone to elementary school. Again, I was shocked that someone who had grown up with me in the same faith community could so something so blatantly prejudiced.

Amid my disappointment in coming across online messages like these from fellow Catholics, I eventually realized that their sentiments were the result of ignorance and fear, not of a conscious, deep-seated hate. The two Catholics in my community who sent these messages, like the other anonymous social media commentators, have likely never had a personal relationship with someone who is Muslim. If they had a Muslim friend, I doubt they would have pressed "Send" or "Tweet." These episodes of Islamophobia in my own community have been hurtful and disappointing, but they are also a reminder of the important role interfaith dialogue and relationship-building can play in breaking down ignorance and fear.

I have not only encountered these kinds of attitudes in the Catholic community I grew up around in Indianapolis, but also among my fellow Christians in the Middle East. When I first moved to Jordan during my junior year of college, I found a country with a long history of interfaith coexistence. My Christian host family's apartment was down the street from the iconic blue King Abdullah mosque, a Coptic church, and a Greek Orthodox church. I often heard church bells and the *adhan*, the Islamic call to prayer, and as I walked down the road on Good Friday in 2012, I heard chanting from the Coptic church meld with the words of the imam's sermon across the street. Jordan is a country that prides itself on interfaith coexistence between Christians and Muslims, who have peacefully lived there together for centuries. Under the surface, though, I noticed that suspicion sometimes brewed.

Like me, my Jordanian host family was Roman Catholic. In the evenings, they often sat down to watch Christian television. I was surprised to find that there were numerous Christian satellite channels, which had Arabic programming and were often produced by Christian groups in the United States or Canada. Many of the Christian programs my host family watched talked often about Islam, attempting to convert viewers. They did so by explaining Christianity, but also by portraying Islam using the same stereotypes and false claims about violence, misogyny, and intolerance that I heard on cable news in the United States. Despite the fact that they lived among Muslims—who are the vast majority of the population in Jordan—my Christian host family bought into these Christian TV channels' negative portrayals of Islam.

On a Saturday afternoon in Amman, two extended family members came over to visit my host family. One of the men was my host mom's adult cousin, and the other was an older Catholic priest who wore a cassock and a big silver cross around his neck. When they learned that I studied Muslim-Christian relations, the conversation quickly turned to Islam.

They spoke of the religion as it was talked about on the Christian programs on TV. To them, the Qur'an and the Prophet Muhammad encouraged violence, mistreatment of women, and oppression of non-Muslims. They asked me if I was aware of writers in the US who warned about the "Islamization" of the West, and encouraged me to read their books. Well acquainted with these writers from my work on Islamophobia, I was shocked that Christians in the Middle East knew of them, too. My host mom turned to me and said, "Muslims are our neighbors, so when we found out about Islam we were shocked. You can read about it online and see videos," she said.

Throughout the conversation, the cousin kept repeating the refrain, "We don't hate Muslims, we just hate Islam." The priest was even less charitable—"I hate both," he said. When he took off his jacket, I noticed he carried a gun, an uncommon thing to see in Amman. Later he said to my nine-year-old host brother, "Never trust a Muslim." Initially stunned after hearing these comments, I eventually went to my room, sat on my bed, and cried. I had never imagined I would find this kind of sentiment in Jordan, especially hearing it so blatantly from a Catholic priest.

This conversation at my Jordanian host family's house hurt me because, as I tried to tell the priest and my host mom, I know people who are Muslim. They are close friends and people who have shaped me in indelible ways. Hearing Muslims talked about this way is upsetting, because—as Nayla Tabbara says—I carry a bit of them with me. This is the experience of spiritual solidarity, Nayla says: "It's as if I am carrying the other's memories, the other's history, the other's hopes and fears with me . . . I carry the hurt of the other with me."[5]

Knowing that my host family had Muslim acquaintances and neighbors, I wondered how they could have such negative views of Muslims and Islam. But, through my time spent with them, and when I eventually returned to Amman to study Muslim-Christian relations the following year, I realized that the relationships they had with Muslims were not all that close or personal. It became clearer to me that in the absence of deep, substantive relationships, the negative media—which seemed more intent on sowing conflict than improving understanding—filled in the void.

Tony Homsy, a young Syrian Jesuit and friend of mine, experienced and observed similar dynamics of mistrust when he was growing up in Syria. Though the country's population is majority Muslim, Tony grew up in a completely Christian neighborhood in Aleppo. He recounted to me that he and his community held on to suspicions and stereotypes about Muslims, even as they encountered Muslims in their daily lives. Tony only started to let go of his negative feelings after finding out that his longtime best friend in school, Bassel, was Muslim. Since then, Tony has fasted twice for the entire month of Ramadan, studied Islam as part of his formation to be a Jesuit, and worked with Muslim children in refugee camps in Lebanon. Tony has received criticism and push-back from his fellow Christians for his positive attitude toward Muslims and Islam.

Tony's experience, and what I witnessed with my host family, are reminders that Christians, like all human beings, can fail in our obligations to be loving and caring. It is easy for us to ascribe the worst intentions to others, and fixate on real (or imagined) wrongs they've committed. Conversely, it is simple for us to ignore our own faults and proudly proclaim the supposed superiority of our beliefs and actions. This triumphalist attitude is not confined to one locale or community; it is something I've encountered in both the United States and the Middle East.

These stories are reminders that dialogue is *not* simply a matter of knowing *of*, or being around, people who are different from us. Dialogue is a *way* of being around, a disposition of being *in relationship* with others. It is about an attitude of openness, allowing others to speak for and define themselves, giving them the benefit of the doubt, assuming the best—not the worst—in others, and refusing to let our ignorance be exploited by those who benefit from conflict. This approach of dialogue is needed in many contexts, regardless of whether Christians are the majority or minority. It is also important for me to say that this dialogical disposition can be lived out even when those of other faiths are not present. I believe that reading this book is a form of being in dialogue with Muslims, albeit in an indirect way.

For me, encountering prejudice toward Muslims in our own Christian communities is one of the most difficult parts of living a Christian life in dialogue with Muslims. It is a sad reminder of the need for the work of building relationships with Muslims, and of carrying our interfaith relationships into our encounters with our fellow Christians. To remedy the fear of Islam that exists in many of our Christian communities, we must testify to the piece of our Muslim friends that we carry inside ourselves.

The Responsibilities: Refusing to Add Another Nail

As he put on his coat and headed toward the door, the Jordanian Catholic priest shook my hand and, with a sinister sarcasm, said, "You take care of those Muslims." I simply nodded and muttered, "Nice to meet you." But I wish I'd answered him differently. My real response should have been, "Yes, I will. I will take care of them."

Just as our religious convictions motivate us to respond to other injustices in our world, our Christian faith compels us to stand against anti-Muslim prejudice, especially in our own communities. *Nostra Aetate*, the Vatican II document on other religions, declares that the church "reproves, as foreign to the mind of Christ, any discrimination against people or any harassment" (5). Yet, we still find prejudice toward Muslims in our communities. An important part of dialogue, Nayla Tabbara insists, is recognizing how our community has wronged others in the past. She explains that the spiritual solidarity resulting from dialogue "means I am no longer on the defensive, I am no longer legitimizing the violence that has been done toward the other group. On the contrary, I am in a place where I take on the responsibility of what has happened in the past from my own group, what my group has inflicted."[6] This means that we must hold our fellow Christians accountable. When we hear a stereotypical or prejudicial comment from a friend, we should kindly express our concern. If we hear something problematic find its way into a sermon or in the petition prayers at Mass on Sunday, we should let our pastor know. As *Nostra Aetate* says, "We cannot truly pray to

God the Father of all if we treat any people as other than sisters and brothers, for all are created in God's image" (5).

For Tony, this is the central truth that guides his dialogue with Muslims. In a conversation we had over email in April 2017, he told me he tries to constantly remember that Muslims, too, are created in God's image, and that the Holy Spirit works in them just as in all others. He is inspired by the love Jesus has for all people, as evidenced by his death on the cross: "The Crucified [Jesus] himself loved everyone equally. In following the message of his life, I try my best not to add another nail to his body by hating my Muslim brothers and sisters."

As a result of our dialogue with Muslims, we as Christians are also called to work with them to make our world a more loving and just place. In *Nostra Aetate*, the church urges us, together with Muslims, to "preserve and promote peace, liberty, social justice and moral values" (3). All over the world, Christians and Muslims have frequently worked together to remedy countless problems and injustices, like poverty, war, and environmental degradation. Like other popes since Vatican II, Pope Francis has often called on Christians and those they dialogue with to "respond to evil with good." This is an echo of God's insistence in the Qur'an: "What is good and what is evil are in no way commensurate. Return evil with something good. In doing so, you will make the one with whom you are at enmity to become like a close friend" (41:34).

Living a life of dialogue also calls us to lift up what we share with Muslims. Through our cooperation and friendship with Muslims, we can demonstrate to the world the many commonalities between our communities and our religions. Together with Muslims, we believe that God is loving and compassionate, that God transcends our understanding and yet is intimately close to us. We strive to cultivate attitudes of gratitude, trust, and patience. We strive to live out God's call to honor and protect the dignity of our fellow human beings, and to bring peace and justice into our world through acts of generous service. Elevating these shared beliefs and values challenges the narrative that our religious communities are in conflict, and sends a powerful witness to the world about the importance of unity despite differences.

Perhaps the most important of the responsibilities of dialogue is to support our Muslim friends' faith lives, their relationship with God. Through dialogue, we begin to learn how our friends relate to God and what their religious practice is like. As Nayla Tabbara describes, we see many beautiful aspects of their tradition, "recognize the richness and authenticity of the other's spiritual experience," and develop an "appreciation" for it.

The church encourages us to support the religious lives of those of other faiths, including Muslims: "Let Christians, while witnessing to their own faith and way of life, *acknowledge, preserve and encourage the spiritual and moral truths found among non-Christians, together with their social life and culture*" (*Nostra Aetate* 2; emphasis mine). The church asserts that I can still remain true to my Catholic identity—that I am in fact living out my Catholicism—while supporting and encouraging my Muslim friends' way of life.

One important way we can do this is by supporting Muslims' prayer. Georgetown, a Catholic university, has a prayer room for student use, complete with a *mihrab*. It isn't big enough to hold the congregational *jum'ah* services with dozens of students on Friday afternoons, but it serves as a spiritual home for Muslim students during the week. DePaul University, another Catholic school, installed an ablutions station so that Muslim students can perform a washing ritual before prayer. In places like Washington, DC, and Tennessee, Christians have also offered their own sanctuaries for Muslims to pray in, especially if there isn't a local mosque or, as has happened in recent years, a mosque has been damaged in arson. At the monastery where Fr. Christian de Chergé lived in Algeria, the brothers turned one of the rooms into a *musallah* for their Muslim guests to pray.

Gestures of spiritual solidarity can be expressed in smaller, everyday ways, too. During Ramadan in the Gaza Strip, a Christian man named Kamal Tarazi helps his friend Hatem Khries, who is blind, get to the mosque five times a day. They also accompany one another to the mosque on Fridays for *jum'ah* and to church on Sundays. I witnessed a similar interfaith friendship in Jordan. On the day after Easter, I accompanied my elderly Muslim neighbor, Najah, to the home of her Christian friend, Leila. This was an annual tradition;

each year they would gather with friends over a big Easter lunch of traditional Jordanian favorites like *mansaf* and *maamoul*. As a gift, Najah brought Leila a shirt with an Arabic poem about Muslim-Christian coexistence printed on it. When it was time for *asr*, the afternoon Islamic prayer, Leila brought out a prayer rug that she keeps in her house for Muslim friends to use when they visit.

Muslims' prayer life is something to be celebrated and encouraged, because it contributes to a deeper relationship with God. Their increased devotion to God is also a gift to Christians, because their example has the potential to draw us closer to God as well.

A Spirit of Communion

At the turn of the twentieth century, a young Frenchman named Louis Massignon traveled to Baghdad in present-day Iraq to do research on a medieval Muslim mystic named al-Hallaj.[7] An agnostic, Massignon had grown up Catholic but no longer practiced the faith. He immersed himself in the language and culture of Baghdad, as well as in the religion of Islam. In a moment of crisis after enduring numerous hardships, Massignon found himself calling upon God—in Arabic. This moment would mark the beginning of his return to Catholicism; eventually he formally converted to the faith and even became a Catholic priest through the Greek, or Melkite, Rite. A scholar of Islam and the founder of the Muslim-Christian *Badaliya* prayer movement, Massignon's writings came to influence the Catholic Church's teachings on Muslims expressed in the Vatican II documents *Lumen Gentium* and *Nostra Aetate*.[8]

During his time as a young man in the Middle East, Massignon was struck by the hospitality he experienced from the Alusis, a Muslim family in Baghdad. The welcome he received from his hosts was a transformative experience that impacted his understanding of God and his attitude toward others. "I was his guest," Massignon wrote of his friend, Ali. "He took me as I was and tried to make me reach my destiny."[9]

In dialogue, we are called to both give and receive what Massignon experienced. We open ourselves to being surprised by how Muslims will help us discover God, and we in turn offer hospitality and spiritual friendship to them. The goal of dialogue is to journey with one another on the path to God, our common destiny.

Interreligious dialogue with Muslims is a threefold blessing. Through our relationships with Muslims, we encounter God in people who we may have previously misunderstood or feared. Through our exposure to Muslims' religion, Islam, we realize that God can be found in many beautiful aspects of a religion that is not our own. And in revisiting our own religion with fresh eyes, we find that God is waiting for us at home, in our own faith tradition, challenging us to live out our Christianity in new ways. These blessings of dialogue with Muslims can also be bestowed through interfaith dialogue with those of any other faith group. I know fellow Christians who have been profoundly shaped by their encounters with Judaism, Hinduism, and other religious traditions. In interfaith dialogue, regardless of who our dialogue partners are, we can find ourselves drawn to God.

This book is meant to be only the first step, the beginning, of a journey of interfaith dialogue with Muslims. In the appendices, I provide guidance for carrying the lessons of this book into one's daily life. There, I offer suggestions for further reading, concrete ideas for engaging with Muslims, and even a prayer that can be used in interfaith settings. As we set off, we should feel confident that the church encourages us in this journey, that dialogue is an inherently Catholic, inherently Christian vocation.

Each of us might take different approaches to living out the "dialogue of life" in our own contexts. But, regardless of our circumstances, we all can begin this journey by attempting to embody what Fr. Frans van der Lugt, a Jesuit priest from the Netherlands, termed "the spirit of *mushaaraka*." Father Frans lived in Syria for fifty years before being killed during the civil war in 2014, and he observed this spirit in the people of Syria, most of whom are Muslim.

A grainy YouTube video uploaded in 2013, just a year before his death, shows Fr. Frans sitting on a small stool in a basalt stone courtyard. Speaking in fluent Arabic with bombs booming in the background, the elderly priest tells the man behind camera that he wants to explain why he loves the Syrian people so much. It's because of their "spirit of *mushaaraka*," he says. He goes on to describe examples of this *mushaaraka* being lived out: a mother in hard circumstances who always makes enough food to share with strangers and neighbors; a host who always gives the guest the best of what she has; and the owner of an orchard who, when he sees young people come by and pick fruit from his trees, encourages it and says, "The property is God's, not mine!"[10]

Mushaaraka, an Arabic word, is hard to translate well into English. "Sharing" gets close; "communion" gets closer. *Mushaaraka* is about choosing to participate in the life of another, engaging in a partnership, which, as Fr. Frans says, "is innate, brotherly, and unguarded, which flows like water from a spring."[11]

Mushaaraka is what the "dialogue of life" is all about. Each of us is called to emulate this free-flowing spirit of communion in our relationships with others, including Muslims. We can do this anywhere in the world—in our neighborhood churches, in the mosque down the street, or in a country across the globe. We should feel confident that wherever we go, God is waiting to greet us. All we must do is be willing to be surprised by God, and open ourselves to witness the sacred in unexpected places. Then, perhaps, we might take off our shoes and find ourselves genuflecting on someone else's holy ground.

To the One, Merciful God be praise and glory for ever. Amen.

—Pope St. John Paul II,
Address to Muslim leaders in Damascus, 2001

وَٱللَّهُ أَعْلَم

In all matters,
God knows best.

Appendix A

Discussion Questions

Organized by chapter, the following questions are intended to prompt discussion of the book in group settings. They could also be a starting point for personal reflection or for writing essays in a classroom context.

Introduction

- The author outlines four types of interfaith dialogue promoted by the Catholic Church—the dialogue of life, the dialogue of religious experience, the dialogue of social action, and the dialogue of theological exchange. Discuss these with your group. Have you participated in one of these forms before? Which one of these would you like to engage in?

- Have you met or do you know someone from a different religious tradition, perhaps someone who is Muslim? Is he or she an acquaintance, friend, or colleague? Discuss your relationship with that person, and what your first impression of him or her was.

- When the author visited the mosque in Cyprus, she felt a sense of reverence and was moved to both cover her head (a Muslim custom) and genuflect (a Catholic custom). Have you visited a house of worship different from your own? How did this space make you feel?

Chapter 1

- Before reading this book, were you aware that Muslims revere the Virgin Mary and that she is discussed in the Qur'an? What do you make of her prominent role in Islam?

- Muslims look to the Prophet Muhammad as an example of how to live a life of goodness and *rahma*, loving mercy. Who in your faith tradition do you look up to, and how do they live out the values and ideals of your faith?

- The author recounted examples of Muslims in her life who serve their communities. Is there someone from another faith tradition whom you admire because of how he or she serves others? This person could be someone you have read about, or whom you know personally.

- The *bismillah* (the phrase, "In the name of God, the Entirely Merciful, the Always Merciful") can be compared to the sign of the cross in Catholicism ("In the name of the Father, and the Son, and the Holy Spirit"). What parallels have you noticed between Christianity and Islam, or other religions you have encountered?

- Discuss the author's comparisons between Jesus and the Qur'an— as the Word of God manifested in creation—and Mary and Muhammad, as sinless vessels who both said "yes" to God.

Chapter 2

- Anti-Muslim prejudice and discrimination have a real impact on people's daily lives. What example of Islamophobia most struck you in this chapter?

- Have you heard of any anti-Muslim incidents reported in the news? How would you feel if this happened to you?

- Have you, your relatives, or your ancestors experienced discrimination because of your religion, ethnicity, or another aspect of your identity? Discuss the parallels between how Muslims are talked about and treated in the United States today and how Catholics, Jews, Japanese Americans, and others have been discriminated against throughout American history.

- The author acknowledges that she has held prejudices toward Muslims. Knowing that we all carry implicit biases about others, how does this make you feel?

- Have your beliefs about Muslims been challenged by what you read in these first two chapters? How might you work to become more aware of your own implicit biases about Muslims?

• What stories or facts presented in these initial chapters will help you to speak up when you hear others express stereotypical or prejudicial views about Muslims?

Chapter 3

• The Islamic call to prayer was something the author appreciated while living in Jordan, because it often drew her into a state of prayer and gratitude. What in your life prompts you to pray? Would hearing the *adhan* or church bells more often in your own life aid your relationship with God?

• *Nostra Aetate*, the Second Vatican Council document on other religions, states that "the Catholic Church rejects nothing of what is true and holy in these religions" and that they "reflect a ray of that truth which enlightens all men and women" (2). If you are Catholic, have you encountered this idea or passage before? What is your reaction to it, and how do you interpret its meaning?

• In the Qur'an, God talks about *ayat*—the "signs" in creation that should remind a person of God. Where do you see God's *ayat* in your life? In interactions with others, nature, music, or prayer?

• Have you ever been moved by something from another faith tradition, like a piece of music, architecture, a ritual, or a line from scripture? Where have you seen the Holy Spirit at work outside of Christianity, in people of other faiths or in aspects of their religion?

Chapter 4

• The Catholic Church teaches that "together with us they [Muslims] adore the one, merciful God" (*Lumen Gentium* 16). What is your reaction to the idea that Christians and Muslims worship the same God?

• Have you prayed with people of another faith? With Muslims specifically? What was this experience like? Would you feel comfortable praying the joint prayer for Christians and Muslims provided on page 121?

• As the author described, both Christians and Muslims describe feeling God's closeness and friendship. When have you felt close to God? What is your relationship to God like?

- The author noted that Christians believe in "original sin," while Muslims don't. What do you make of this? How do theological differences like this impact our relationships with Muslims?

Chapter 5

- The author described her faith journey, growing up in Catholicism, exploring other religions like Islam, and finding a home again in Christianity. What have been some pivotal moments in your own faith journey?

- Many Muslims pray five times daily. How would your relationship with God change if you spent five to ten minutes in prayer five times each day? What sacrifices would you have to make to do this?

- What does "salvation" mean to you? When you imagine heaven, what is it like? What is your reaction to the Catholic Church's teaching that the "plan of salvation" includes those who aren't Christian?

- How have conversations with people of other faiths helped you reflect more deeply on your own religious beliefs? Did they prompt you to view an aspect of your faith in a new way?

Chapter 6

- If you have had the opportunity to participate in interfaith dialogue before, what have been its rewards in your own life?

- The author discusses experiences where people in her own community have made hurtful comments about Muslims. Have you witnessed or heard about instances like this in your community? How did you react or respond?

- One of the author's favorite Qur'anic passages is this prayer of Moses:

  Oh Lord, open my heart
  Make my task easy for me,
  Undo the knot of my tongue
  So that they may understand what I have to say. (20:25-28)

Spend some time contemplating this prayer. What does it say to you? Do you have a favorite prayer or passage from the Bible or another scriptural text that motivates or comforts you in your own life?

- The author talked about the importance of concepts like "spiritual solidarity" and "*mushaaraka.*" How might these ideas shape the way you live the "dialogue of life" in your own community?

- After reading this book, what do you want to do now? Is there a particular message you want to share with your community, or a particular action you want to take? How might you live out your faith differently as a result?

Appendix B

Guidelines for Dialogue with Muslims

Getting to Know Muslims

After reading this book, many readers may want to know how they can reach out to Muslims in their community. Muslims live throughout the United States. Find out if your city has a local interfaith organization or university that hosts events where you can learn about Islam or get to know Muslims. Mosques and Muslim student groups at colleges often host events that are open to the public. Following local groups' Facebook pages is a great way to see what events are coming up in your area. During the Islamic month of Ramadan, consider attending an interfaith *iftar*.

Simply striking up a conversation with a Muslim colleague, neighbor, classmate, or parent at your child's school can go a long way. Consider inviting him or her to get coffee or organize a playdate with your kids. Your reaching out, especially amid a climate of increased anti-Muslim prejudice, will be very much appreciated. But be cognizant not to overburden the Muslims you meet with countless activities and requests—remember, they have busy lives, too! Still, making contact is always a kind and welcome gesture.

Regardless of what your outreach looks like, the most important thing to remember is that Muslims are just like everybody else.

Social media is also a great way to get to know Muslims. There are a number of North American Muslim leaders who you might consider following on Facebook or Twitter:

- Omid Safi
- Ingrid Mattson
- Imam Khalid Latif
- Jerusha Lamptey
- Tarek El-Messidi
- Hind Makki
- Eboo Patel
- Sheikh Omar Suleiman
- Amanda Saab
- Alaa Murabit
- Kameelah Rashad
- Rep. Keith Ellison
- Zareena Grewal
- Imam Yahya Hendi

There are also a number of storytelling initiatives, nonprofit organizations, and educational institutions that you can follow online to better understand the issues that Muslims are talking about and that impact their lives:

- The Bridge Initiative at Georgetown University
- Duke Islamic Studies Center
- Muslim Writers Collective
- *The Secret Life of Muslims*
- Shoulder to Shoulder Campaign
- Yaqeen Institute for Islamic Research

Planning a Gathering

Hosting an event with Muslims can be a meaningful experience for all involved. The first and most important step is to let the Muslim community in your area know you want to be supportive of them; then, ask *them* how you can help. Here are some potential event ideas:

- an *iftar* dinner during Ramadan for the local Muslim community
- a public talk on Islam or Islamophobia from a local expert

- a joint community service activity
- a spoken-word event where Muslim individuals can share about their experiences
- a film screening followed by small-group discussions

These are just some ideas, and they can easily be combined. Here are a few things to keep in mind, regardless of the type of event you put together:

- If Islamic prayer times fall during your event, schedule prayer time into the program. (You can find the prayer times for your location through a simple Google search.) If you can, offer a quiet room for folks to pray in, and provide some prayer rugs. If you want to watch the *salah* prayer, ask your guests if they'd be OK with that and where you should stand.

- Like many Jews, most Muslims don't eat pork products. To be respectful of this dietary norm, avoid serving pork products (including things like gelatin). Additionally, many Muslims only eat meat that is *halal* or "permissible," meaning that the animal was killed in a humane and healthy way, and with an invocation of God. So if you want to serve meat at your event, speak to your Muslim contacts and cater from a restaurant that prepares *halal* meat. Or go meatless and serve a vegetarian meal!

- Most Muslims don't drink alcohol, and Islamic norms prohibit it, so save the beer and wine for another time. Out of respect, don't host your event in a venue like a bar.

Having the local Muslim community involved throughout the planning process will help make your event be a success for both your community and theirs.

Topics for Dialogue

If you want to have an event that involves reflection and conversation, pair it with an activity—like a dinner or movie screening—that can provide a topic for discussion. If you do a joint community service activity, for example, ask participants to talk about what in their own faith inspires them to serve others. Here are some other ideas for discussion:

- God's attributes, like mercy/*rahma*
- Jesus, Mary, and other religious role models
- pilgrimage and holy sites
- mysticism and poetry
- forms of prayer

One of my favorite prompting questions for interfaith dialogue is this: What is your relationship with God like? This is a simple question but one that facilitates reflection and personal conversation.

Regardless of the topic, consider writing up some dialogue ground rules for participants, like these:

- Speak in the first person about your own experiences, using "I" statements.
- Don't interrupt others, and listen openly to them.
- Interpret another's words in the most positive light and remember to assume they have good intentions.
- Don't expect others to represent the whole of their religion, but, at the same time, recognize that their voice is an authentic one.
- Before you pose a question to a person of another faith, answer it yourself first. (This process will help you not only learn about the other, but also about yourself.)

Visiting a Mosque

If you want to go to a mosque, reach out to the local community to see what opportunities there are for you to visit. When you go, be prepared to take off your shoes in the sanctuary. Both men and women should dress modestly, and women should be prepared to wear a scarf over their hair. Women can bring a scarf with them, but oftentimes the mosque will provide them. Remember that you're in a holy space, and act reverently as you would in your own house of worship.

Most mosques welcome visitors for the weekly Friday service. If you go, expect the formal congregational *salah* prayer, followed by a sermon.

Praying for Muslims

Does your congregation ever pray specifically for people of other faiths? If not, consider adding a prayer for Muslims or people of other faiths into the petition prayers in your church service. Also consider praying for an end to religious discrimination, and for the strength and courage for all of us to be aware of and confront our own prejudices.

Showing Support and Standing Up

Islamophobia is not a problem Muslims should be expected to solve; rather, it is the responsibility of non-Muslims to dismantle. There are many actions you can take to show your support for Muslims and others impacted by racism and religious discrimination:

- Write an op-ed for your local newspaper or school publication.
- Make a public gesture by putting up signs or posters.
- Urge government officials to adopt fair and just policies.
- Educate yourself and others (using some of the resources recommended in this book).
- Charitably confront prejudice and discrimination when you witness it, whether on social media, in your community, or even at your church. (If you see someone who is being harassed in public, try not to engage the perpetrator, but rather start a conversation with the victim and accompany him or her to a safe space, if you can. Pretend to know the victim, and say, "Hey, sorry I was late!" or "Hey, it's good to run into you!" and the person harassing will likely move along.)

Again, ask your Muslim friends how you can help. The best ally you can be is the one your Muslim friends need you to be.

Appendix C

A Joint Prayer for Christians and Muslims

Merciful and Compassionate God,[1]
Who created humanity in unity and diversity:[2]
Help us to be peacemakers[3]
And inspire us to repel evil with good.[4]
Help us to love our neighbors,[5]
To welcome the stranger,[6]
And to turn enemies into friends.[7]
Guide us as one community[8]
As we strive on the path of justice, peace, and understanding.[9]
Amen.

(This prayer was composed by the author, and is adapted from an earlier version published online in *Sojourners*. It is intended for use by Christians and Muslims, who can pray it together. It incorporates scripture and teachings from both Islamic and Christian traditions, and affirms the common values shared by those who recite it.)

Appendix D

Resources for Further Study

The following is a list of books and articles that are recommended for additional reading. More online resources are listed in appendix B, under the heading "Getting to Know Muslims," as well.

Islam: Overviews of the Faith

The Fragrance of Faith: The Enlightened Heart of Islam by Jamal Rahman

Following Muhammad: Rethinking Islam in the Contemporary World by Carl W. Ernst

Meeting Islam: A Guide for Christians by George Dardess

The Vision of Islam by Sachiko Murata and William Chittick

The Qur'an

How to Read the Qur'an: A New Guide, with Select Translations by Carl W. Ernst

Readings in the Qur'ān by Kenneth Cragg, a compilation of Qur'anic passages organized by theme

Qur'an in Conversation by Michael Birkel (editor)

The Study Quran: A New Translation and Commentary by Seyyed Hossein Nasr, Caner K. Dagli, Maria Massi Dakake, Joseph E. B. Lumbard, Mohammed Rustom (editors)

The Story of the Qur'an: Its History and Place in Muslim Life by Ingrid Mattson

Muhammad & Jesus

Memories of Muhammad: Why the Prophet Matters by Omid Safi
Muhammad: A Very Short Introduction by Jonathan A. C. Brown
The Muslim Jesus: Sayings and Stories in Islamic Literature by
   Tarif Khalidi

Islamic Spirituality & Theology

Essential Sufism by James Fadiman and Robert Frager (editors),
   a book of poetry and sayings
*Seven Doors to Islam: Spirituality and the Religious Life of
   Muslims* by John Renard
"Divine and Human Love in Islam" by William Chittick in *Divine
   Love: Perspectives from the World's Religious Traditions*, edited
   by Jeff Levin and Stephen G. Post

Interfaith Dialogue & Muslim-Christian Relations

Nostra Aetate (In Our Time), Declaration on the Relation of the
   Church to Non-Christian Religions
Divine Hospitality: A Christian-Muslim Conversation by Fadi
   Daou and Nayla Tabbara
Of Gods and Men by Xavier Beauvois (director), a film about
   Fr. Christian de Chergé and his fellow monks
*The Saint and the Sultan: The Crusades, Islam, and Francis of
   Assisi's Mission of Peace* by Paul Moses
*A Common Word: Muslims and Christians on Loving God and
   Neighbor* by Miroslav Volf, Ghazi bin Muhammad, and Melissa
   Yarrington (editors)
*Islam and Christianity: Theological Themes in Comparative
   Perspective* by John Renard
A History of Christian-Muslim Relations by Hugh Goddard
Christian de Chergé: A Theology of Hope by Christian Salenson
"*Nostra Aetate* and the Questions It Chose to Leave Open" by
   Daniel Madigan in *Gregorianum* 87.4

Autobiographies & Biographies

The Bread of Angels: A Journey to Love and Faith by Stephanie Saldaña

If the Oceans Were Ink: An Unlikely Friendship and a Journey to the Heart of the Quran by Carla Power

The Monks of Tibhirine: Faith, Love, and Terror in Algeria by John W. Kiser

Islamophobia & Islam in America

American Heretics: Catholics, Jews, Muslims, and the History of Religious Intolerance by Peter Gottschalk

"Danger & Dialogue: American Catholic Public Opinion and Portrayals of Islam" by Jordan Denari Duffner, report from the Bridge Initiative at Georgetown University

Muslims and the Making of America by Amir Hussain

Appendix E

Glossary

ablutions: Ritual washing before prayer that is a practice in many religions. In Islam, Muslims wash their faces, hands, and feet before prayer.

adhan: Pronounced "a-thaan," the "call to prayer" is recited in Arabic before *salah*, Islamic ritual prayer. In many places, it is recited publicly from a tower called a minaret or over a loudspeaker.

agape: The Greek word in the New Testament that describes God's self-giving love for humanity.

al-asmaa al-husna: God's ninety-nine "beautiful names" in Arabic.

Algeria: A Muslim-majority country in North Africa colonized by France for over one hundred years. It saw a brutal civil war in the 1990s.

Alhamdulillah: "Praise be to God" or "Hallelujah" in Arabic.

al-Khabeer: "The One who knows you best," or "the Well-Acquainted." One of Islam's ninety-nine attributes for God.

Allah: "God" in Arabic.

Allahu akbar: "God is greater" or "God is the greatest" in Arabic. Recited during the Islamic call to prayer, or used as an expression to invoke God.

al-Latif: "The Kindest One," one of Islam's ninety-nine attributes for God.

al-Wadud: "The Affectionate," or "the Loving," one of Islam's ninety-nine attributes for God.

Amman: The capital city of Jordan.

apse: A curved inlet in churches, usually at the front of the sanctuary.

Arab: A person who speaks the Arabic language. Also an adjective to describe parts of the world where Arabic is the primary language spoken. "Arab" should not be confused with "Muslim." In the United States, the majority of Arab Americans are Christian, not Muslim.

Arabic: A Semitic language related to Hebrew spoken by at least 290 million people in many parts of the Middle East and North Africa including Muslims, Christians, Jews, Druze, and others. Arabic is also the language of the Qur'an, which is the Word of God for Muslims. Thus, many Muslims who are nonnative Arabic speakers use the language as a part of religious practice.

Aramaic: A Semitic language spoken by Jews during the time of Jesus. Related to Arabic and Hebrew.

ar-Rahim: An attribute of God, meaning "the Always Merciful." Often paired with *ar-Rahman* in the *bismillah*.

ar-Rahman: Literally, "the Entirely Merciful," it is the defining attribute of God in Islam. It is also the title of a chapter of the Qur'an.

asr: The afternoon Islamic *salah* prayer time.

Augustine of Hippo: A fourth-century bishop, saint, and Christian theologian whose writings shaped Western Christianity.

ayat: Plural for the "signs" of God. Also used to refer to the verses of the Qur'an. (Singular, *ayah*.)

Bismillah ar-Rahman ar-Rahim: The Arabic formula of consecration used by Muslims to begin prayer or other tasks. Literally, "In the name of God, the Entirely Merciful, the Always Merciful," it appears at the beginning of all but one of the chapters of the Qur'an.

Carmelite: A priest, brother, nun, or layperson belonging to the Catholic, Carmelite religious orders.

chaplains: Religious leaders who serve at universities, hospitals, or in the military to accompany and support those in these institutions.

Christian de Chergé: A Catholic monk who devoted his life to living in dialogue with Muslims in Algeria. He and several other Cistercian monks were murdered in 1996.

Cistercian: A member of a Catholic religious order that follows the Rule of St. Benedict.

Cyprus: An island country in the eastern Mediterranean Sea.

dhikr: Pronounced "zikr" or "thicker." Literally, "repetition" or "remembrance" in Arabic, it is the practice of recalling God, often through recitation of Qur'anic verses.

dinar: The monetary currency in some countries, including Jordan.

dua: A petition prayer in Islam.

Eucharist: The consecrated bread and wine that Catholics believe is the Body and Blood of Jesus Christ.

fitra: The original, primordial state of each human soul, according to Islam. *Fitra* is the soul's predisposition to goodness, to know God and submit to God's will, the quality of being in harmony with God and the rest of creation.

Francis of Assisi: A thirteenth-century Roman Catholic saint, who visited the Egyptian Muslim leader Sultan Malik al-Kamil during the Crusades.

genuflection: To drop down onto one's right knee and make the sign of the cross. A common practice for Catholics and other Christians when approaching the Eucharist.

hadith: A saying of the Prophet Muhammad. The prophet's sayings and example are considered a second source of scripture for Muslims after the Qur'an.

hajj: An annual pilgrimage to Mecca that all Muslims endeavor to make once during their lifetime. It involves numerous rituals, including circling around the *ka'aba* in prayer.

hijab: Literally "covering," it is often used to describe the headscarf worn by many Muslim women. *Hijab* is also used to refer to the general ethic of modesty.

holy envy: A term coined by Krister Stendahl for a person's admiration of something of another religious tradition and wanting something like it in one's own tradition.

hubb: An Arabic word for "love" or "like."

Ibn Arabi: A Muslim mystic, philosopher, and poet, known as the "Greatest Master," who died in the thirteenth century.

iftar: A fast-breaking meal, often during Ramadan.

imam: A person who leads Islamic *salah* prayer. Literally means "in front."

Isa: The Arabic name for Jesus used by Muslims.

isha: The nighttime Islamic *salah* prayer time.

ishq: An Arabic word for love in Islamic mystical poetry.

Islam: The religion of Muslims. In Arabic, the word is related to "peace," and connotes giving one's self over to God.

Islamic: An adjective used in English to describe inanimate things related to the religion of Islam, like history, art, or a community center. (A practitioner of Islam is not "an Islamic" or an "Islamic person," but rather a "Muslim." The word "Islamic" is the linguistic equivalent to "Judaic," not "Jewish.")

Islamophobia: Prejudice toward or discrimination against people for their perceived association with the religion of Islam.

Jabal al-Weibdeh: A historic neighborhood in central Amman.

Jerusalem: A city in the Middle East considered to be holy by Jews, Christians, and Muslims.

Jesuit: A priest or brother of the Society of Jesus, a male Catholic religious order founded by St. Ignatius of Loyola.

Jordan: An Arabic-speaking country in the Levant region of the Middle East. Most of its 8 million residents practice the religion of Islam.

The Joy of the Gospel *(Evangelii Gaudium)*: A 2013 apostolic exhortation by Pope Francis.

jum'ah: The congregational Friday prayer service for Muslims, often held at a mosque.

ka'aba: The sacred "house of God" on earth for Muslims. Muslims face the *ka'aba* during prayer and it is the main site visited during pilgrimage, or *hajj*.

Laudato Sì: Pope Francis's encyclical on caring for creation, in which he cited a Muslim mystic.

Levant: A region of the Middle East that usually refers to Lebanon, Syria, Jordan, and Israel-Palestine.

Lumen Gentium: The Dogmatic Constitution on the Catholic Church released during the Second Vatican Council in 1965.

maghrib: "Sunset" in Arabic. One of the five times many Muslims pray *salah*.

Magnificat: Known as the "Song of Mary," it is a prayer recited by the Virgin Mary in the Gospel of Luke.

Malik al-Kamil: A sultan of the Muslim Ayyubid dynasty who met with St. Francis of Assisi during the Crusades.

marhoum: Someone who has passed away, literally, "someone upon whom there is mercy" in Arabic.

Maryam: Arabic for "Mary." In Islam, Mary is also revered as the mother of Jesus.

masbaha: Islamic prayer beads, similar to a rosary.

Mass: A Catholic Church service in which the Eucharist is celebrated.

Mecca: The birthplace of Muhammad, and location of the *ka'aba*, the focal point of Muslims' prayer. Mecca is the holiest city for Muslims, and millions go on pilgrimage, or *hajj*, there every year.

Medina: The second most important holy city for Muslims. Literally, "the city" in Arabic, and short for "the city of the prophet." The Prophet Muhammad and his community emigrated there after facing persecution in Mecca. Muhammad is buried in Medina, and it is also a site of pilgrimage.

Middle East: A loosely defined region of Western Asia, usually stretching from the Mediterranean Sea through Iran. It is not synonymous with the "Arab world," since countries like Iran are not primarily Arabic-speaking.

mihrab: A curved inlet that serves as the focal point in all mosques, pointing to the direction of the *ka'aba* in Mecca.

mosque: A house of worship for Muslims. In Arabic, *masjid*, which literally means "place of prostration."

Muhammad: The last prophet in Islam. Literally, "praiseworthy" in Arabic.

musallah: A Muslim prayer room, literally, "place of *salah*."

mushaaraka: An Arabic word for "sharing," "participation," or "communion."

Muslim: A follower of the religion of Islam. Related to the Arabic word for peace, it refers to someone who devotes oneself to God. There are over 1.6 billion Muslims, who live in all parts of the world.

Negus: An Ethiopian Christian king who welcomed Muslims who were fleeing Mecca during the time of the Prophet Muhammad.

nia: "Intention" in Arabic.

Nostra Aetate: The Catholic Church's declaration about other religions, released during the Second Vatican Council in 1965.

Qur'an: The Word of God and holiest text for Muslims. Literally, "recitation" or "reading aloud." The divine revelations that make up the Qur'an were communicated to the Prophet Muhammad over a span of twenty-three years.

rahma: God's defining quality in Islam. It means "mercy," "compassion," and "loving-kindness," and is associated with a mother's love for the child of her womb.

Ramadan: The ninth month of the Islamic lunar calendar. During this time, Muslims fast from food and drink from dawn to sunset. The month ends with one of the two most important Islamic holidays, *Eid al-Fitr*, or "the Feast of Fast-breaking."

Rumi: A famous Muslim mystic and poet of the thirteenth century.

salah: A ritual form of Islamic prayer that most Muslims do five times daily. It combines passages of the Qur'an with movement of the body.

Sayyidat al-Jabal: A holy shrine in northern Jordan dedicated to the Virgin Mary where miracles have been reported. Literally, "Our Lady of the Mount."

Sayyidatuna: "Our Lady" in Arabic. A reverent way to refer to Mary, the mother of Jesus.

Second Vatican Council, or Vatican II: A council of bishops in the mid-1960s in which the Catholic Church experienced *aggiornamento*, or "updating."

Semitic languages: A family of languages spoken in parts of the Middle East and Africa.

sujuud: Arabic for "prostration."

Surat al-Fatiha: Literally, "the Opening Chapter," this chapter begins the Qur'an and is included in every *salah* prayer. It plays a central role in Muslims' prayer life.

Umm Haram: A seventh-century woman who was the aunt of Islam's Prophet Muhammad. Her name means "honorable mother."

umma: "Community" in Arabic. Often used to refer to the global Muslim community today.

Zamzam: Holy water from a well in Mecca.

Appendix F

Pronunciations and Definitions of Select Given Names

Aamina: AH-mina: *"trustworthy," the name of the Prophet Muhammad's mother*

Aamir: AH-mir: *"prosperous," "full of life"*

Abdelkader: abdel-QAH-dir: *"servant of the powerful"*

Abdullah: abd-UHL-lah: *"servant of God"*

Ahmed: AH-med: *"most praised," another name for Muhammad*

Ali, or Aly: AAH-LEE: *"high," "elevated"*

Aseel: ah-SEAL: *"pure," "noble"*

Asima: AH-sim-ah: *"guardian," "protector"*

Ayah: EYE-YAH: *"sign," "miracle (from God)"*

Bassel: BA-sil: *"bold"*

Deah: dee-YEAH: *"light"*

Elhan: il-HAN: *"inspiration"*

Fadi: FAA-di: *"redeemer," usually a name for Christians*

Hanna: HAN-nah: *"John," usually a name for Christians (Yahya for "John" is common among Muslims)*

Hassan: HA-SAN: *"handsome," "good," one of the prophet's two grandsons*

Hatem: HA-tim: *"determined"*

Hossein, or Hussain: who-SAYN: *"handsome," "good," one of the prophet's two grandsons*

Isa, or Issa: *"Jesus"*

Jaafar: JAA-far: *"spring (of water)"*

Kamal: ka-MAAL: *"perfection," "completeness"*

Kamil: KAA-mil: *"perfect," "complete"*

Khadr, or Khidr: KHAD-r: literally, *"the green,"* the name of a Muslim prophet or St. George

Khalid: KHA-lid: *"eternal"*

Leila: LAY-la: *"night"*

Maryam: MAR-ee-yum: *"Mary"*

Muhammad, or Mohamed: mo-HAMM-ad: *"one who is praised,"* the name of Muslims' last prophet

Muneeb: moo-NEEB: *"one who turns in repentance"*

Nadir: NAH-dir: *"rare," "dear"*

Najah: na-JAAH: *"success"*

Nayla: NAY-lah: *"one who succeeds"*

Nazir: na-ZEER: *"warner"*

Omid: oh-MEED: *"hope"*

Osama: oo-SA-mah: *"lion"*

Rabieh: ra-BEE-a: *"spring"* (the season)

Razan: ra-ZAAN: *"serenity"*

Reema: REE-ma: *"white antelope"*

Talib: TAH-lib: *"student," "one who asks"*

Walead, or Waleed, or Walid: wa-LEED: *"newborn"*

Wardah: WAR-tha (or WAR-deh): *"rose"*

Yusor: YUH-sore: *"ease"*

Zeyneb, or Zainab: ZAY-nab: *"father's precious jewel,"* name of one of the Prophet Muhammad's daughters

Notes

Introduction

[1] "Article VI. The Story of Umm Haram," *Journal of the Royal Asiatic Society of Great Britain & Ireland*, edited in the original Turkish and translated by Claude Delaval Cobham (Cambridge University Press for the Royal Asiatic Society, 1897).

[2] Vatican Secretariat for Non-Christians, The Attitude of the Church toward the Followers of Other Religions: Reflections and Orientations on Dialogue and Mission (Vatican City: Libreria Editrice Vaticana, Pentecost 1984), 2–3.

[3] Michael L. Fitzgerald, "Pope John Paul II and Interreligious Dialogue," *L'Osservatore Romano*, May 25, 2005, http://www.ewtn.com/library/chistory /intrejp2.htm.

[4] Vatican Secretariat for Non-Christians, The Attitude of the Church toward the Followers of Other Religions, 13.

[5] Christian de Chergé, *L'invincible espérance*, ed. Bruno Chenu (Paris: Bayard, 1996), 183–84; quoted in Christian Salenson, *Christian de Chergé: A Theology of Hope* (Collegeville, MN: Cistercian Publications, 2012), 50.

[6] de Chergé, *L'invincible espérance*, 74; quoted in Salenson, *Christian de Chergé*, 49.

[7] Vatican Secretariat for Non-Christians, The Attitude of the Church toward the Followers of Other Religions, 42.

[8] Thomas Ryan, "Proclamation and Dialogue: Partner Expressions of Evangelization," Paulist Office for Ecumenical and Interfaith Relations, http://tomryancsp.org/proclamation.htm.

[9] Vatican Secretariat for Non-Christians, The Attitude of the Church toward the Followers of Other Religions, 37.

[10] Ibid., 3.

[11] Francis, Audience with the Diplomatic Corps Accredited to the Holy See, Vatican website, March 22, 2013, http://w2.vatican.va/content/francesco /en/speeches/2013/march/documents/papa-francesco_20130322_corpo -diplomatico.html.

[12] Jordan Denari Duffner, "Danger and Dialogue: American Catholic Public Opinion and Portrayals of Islam," The Bridge Initiative, http://bridge .georgetown.edu/wp-content/uploads/2016/09/Bridge_CathReport_Single .pdf.

[13] Francis, *Evangelii Gaudium* (The Joy of the Gospel) 253, Vatican website, November 24, 2013, http://w2.vatican.va/content/francesco/en /apost_exhortations/documents/papa-francesco_esortazione-ap_20131124 _evangelii-gaudium.html.

Chapter 1

[1] Marialaura Conte, "Lebanon: How the Annunciation came to be a joint Muslim-Christian national holiday," interview with Mohamad Nokkari, *Oasis*, March 29, 2010, http://www.oasiscenter.eu/articles/interreligious -dialogue/2010/03/29/lebanon-how-the-annunciation-came-to-be-a-joint -muslim-christian-national-holiday.

[2] Los Angeles Lakers, "Student and Educators for the month of February 2015," http://www.nba.com/lakers/community/1415_seom.

[3] See Hadith 13, "40 Hadith Nawawi," Sunnah.com, https://sunnah. com/nawawi40/13. (Note: This source is a popular compilation of forty of the Prophet Muhammad's sayings, most of which come from the *hadith* compilations of Sahih al-Bukhari and Sahih Muslim.)

[4] Yara Bishara, "Who Are the White Helmets?," *New York Times*, February 27, 2017, https://www.nytimes.com/video/world/middleeast /100000004695192/white-helmets-syria.html.

[5] "Rebuild with Love: Rebuild Black Churches & Support Victims of Arson across the South," LaunchGood, https://www.launchgood.com /project/rebuild_with_love_rebuild_black_churches_support_victims_of _arson_across_the_south#/.

[6] Vatican Radio, "Pakistan: Muslim villagers donate money to build a Church," *Vatican Radio*, June 15, 2016, http://en.radiovaticana.va/news /2016/06/15/pakistan_muslim_villagers_donate_money_to_build_a_church _/1237380.

[7] Imam Zaid Shakir's Facebook page, photo, October 12, 2016, https:// www.facebook.com/imamzaidshakir/photos/a.10151919830963359 .1073741831.17621258358/10153966510543359/?type=3.

[8] Tomorrow, Inshallah Facebook page, post, December 5, 2016, https:// www.facebook.com/TomorrowInshallah/posts/354539324906347:0.

[9] Carol Kuruvilla, "Here are 4 Concepts in Islam Muslims Wish You'd Talk About More," *Huffington Post*, April 6, 2016, http://www.huffingtonpost .com/entry/here-are-4-concepts-in-islam-muslims-wish-youd-talk-about -more_us_57054f17e4b0537661887c73.

[10] Imam Talib Shareef, Speech, Interfaith iftar, Washington, DC, June 2016.

[11] Imam Yahya Hendi (director for Muslim Life at Georgetown University), in discussion with the author, April 2017.

[12] Sahih al-Bukhari, "Prophetic Commentary on the Qur'an (Tafseer of the Prophet [pbuh])," Vol. 6, Book 60, Hadith 227, Sunnah.com, https: //sunnah.com/urn/43820.

[13] Kais Dukes, "Verb (form I)—to have mercy," Quran Dictionary, http: //corpus.quran.com/qurandictionary.jsp?q=rHm.

[14] Todd Lawson, "Divine Wrath and Divine Mercy in Islam," in *Divine Wrath and Divine Mercy in the World of Antiquity*, ed. Reinhard G. Kratz and Hermann Spieckermann, 248–67 (Tübingen, Germany: Mohr Siebeck, 2008), http://toddlawson.ca/pdf/lawson_divine_wrath.pdf.

[15] Walter Kasper, *Mercy: The Essence of the Gospel and the Key to Christian Life* (New York/Mahwah, NJ: Paulist Press, 2013), 42.

[16] Sahih Muslim, "The Book of Repentance," Book 50, Hadith 25, https://sunnah.com/muslim/50/25.

[17] Reza Shah-Kazemi, "God, 'The Loving,'" in *A Common Word: Muslims and Christians on Loving God and Neighbor*, ed. Miroslav Volf, Ghazi bin Muhammad, and Melissa Yarrington, 105 (Grand Rapids, MI: Eerdmans, 2010).

[18] Riyad as-Salihin, "The Book of Miscellany," Book 1, Hadith 419, https://sunnah.com/riyadussaliheen/1/419.

[19] Francis, *The Church of Mercy*, quoted in "Pope Francis on the Parable of the Merciful Father," LoyolaPress.com, http://www.loyolapress.com/our-catholic-faith/scripture-and-tradition/catholic-living/pope-francis-on-the-parable-of-the-merciful-father.

[20] Riyad as-Salihin, "The Book of Miscellany," Book 1, Hadith 96, https://sunnah.com/riyadussaliheen/1/96. (Note: translation has been altered for clarity.)

[21] Francis, Address of His Holiness Pope Francis to Representatives of Different Religions, Vatican website, November 3, 2016, https://w2.vatican.va/content/francesco/en/speeches/2016/november/documents/papa-francesco_20161103_udienza-interreligiosa.html.

[22] Kasper, *Mercy*, 83.

[23] Mahmoud Ayoub, *The Qur'an and Its Interpreters: Volume 2: The House of 'Imran* (Albany, NY: State University of New York Press, 1992), 275.

[24] Carl Ernst, *Following Muhammad: Rethinking Islam in the Contemporary World* (Chapel Hill: University of North Carolina Press, 2004), 86.

[25] Walead Mosaad, "Giving Life to Surat al-Kahf," *Islam for Life*, podcast, October 29, 2016, https://www.youtube.com/watch?v=W4GGv30C37I.

[26] Wardah Khalid, Twitter post, December 24, 2016, https://twitter.com/wardahkhalid_/status/812701660862676992.

[27] Jonathan A. C. Brown, *Muhammad: A Very Short Introduction* (New York: Oxford University Press, 2011), 10.

[28] Daniel Madigan, "Nostra Aetate and the questions it chose to leave open," *Gregorianum* 87, no. 4 (2006): 793.

[29] *Nostra Aetate* (Declaration on the Relation of the Church to Non-Christian Religions) 3. Quotations of Vatican II documents are taken from Austin Flannery, ed., *Vatican Council II: The Basic Sixteen Documents* (Collegeville, MN: Liturgical Press, 1996).

[30] Qur'an 15:29; 32:9; 38:72.

Chapter 2

[1] "Mosque Leader Wants Hate Crime Charge for Man Held in Pellet Gun Attack," *CBS Chicago*, August 12, 2012, http://chicago.cbslocal.com/2012/08/12/man-charged-with-firing-pellet-rifle-at-morton-grove-mosque/.

[2] Francis, *Evangelii Gaudium* (The Joy of the Gospel) 253, Vatican website, November 24, 2013, http://w2.vatican.va/content/francesco/en

/apost_exhortations/documents/papa-francesco_esortazione-ap_20131124
_evangelii-gaudium.html.

³ Sandy Hingston, "Bullets and Bigots: Remembering Philadelphia's 1844 Anti-Catholic Riots," *Philadelphia Magazine*, December 17, 2015, http://www.phillymag.com/news/2015/12/17/philadelphia-anti-catholic-riots-1844/.

⁴ Thomas Nast, *The American River Ganges*, 1875, Wikimedia Commons, https://commons.wikimedia.org/wiki/File:The_American_River_Ganges_(Thomas_Nast_cartoon).jpg.

⁵ Stephan Salisbury, "Interfaith effort works to beautify Philadelphia mosque," *Philly.com*, January 10, 2016, http://www.philly.com/philly/news/20160110_Interfaith_effort_works_to_beautify_Philadelphia_mosque.html.

⁶ Thomas Whitney, *A defence of the American policy, as opposed to the encroachments of foreign influence, and especially to the interference of the papacy in the political interests and affairs of the United States* (1856), 79–80, http://quod.lib.umich.edu/m/moa/ahm4910.0001.001/79?page=root;rgn=full+text;size=100;view=image.

⁷ Salisbury, "Interfaith effort works to beautify Philadelphia mosque."

⁸ Jessica Taylor, "Trump Calls for 'Total and Complete Shutdown of Muslims Entering' U.S.," *NPR*, December 7, 2015, http://www.npr.org/2015/12/07/458836388/trump-calls-for-total-and-complete-shutdown-of-muslims-entering-u-s.

⁹ Julie Des Jardins, "From Citizen to Enemy: The Tragedy of Japanese Internment," The Gilder Lehrman Institute of American History, https://www.gilderlehrman.org/history-by-era/world-war-ii/essays/from-citizen-enemy-tragedy-japanese-internment; T.A. Frail, "The Injustice of Japanese-American Internment Camps Resonates Strongly to This Day," *Smithsonian Magazine*, January 2017, http://www.smithsonianmag.com/history/injustice-japanese-americans-internment-camps-resonates-strongly-180961422/.

¹⁰ Chris Rickerd, "Homeland Security Suspends Ineffective, Discriminatory Immigration Program," ACLU, May 6, 2011, https://www.aclu.org/blog/speakeasy/homeland-security-suspends-ineffective-discriminatory-immigration-program.

¹¹ Arjun Sethi, "9/11 was 15 years ago. Why do so many of us feel less safe?," *The Guardian*, September 8, 2016, https://www.theguardian.com/commentisfree/2016/sep/08/9-11-us-safety-ethnic-racial-religious-profiling.

¹² United States Holocaust Memorial Museum, "United States Policy Toward Jewish Refugees, 1941–1952," https://www.ushmm.org/wlc/en/article.php?ModuleId=10007094.

¹³ Azadeh Ansari, "FBI: Hate crimes spike, most sharply against Muslims," *CNN*, November 15, 2016, http://www.cnn.com/2016/11/14/us/fbi-hate-crime-report-muslims/.

¹⁴ "The First 9/11 Backlash Fatality: The Murder of Balbir Singh Sodhi," Sikh American Legal Defense and Education Fund, August 30, 2011, http://saldef.org/issues/balbir-singh-sodhi/#.WO4eUhLys3g.

¹⁵ Michael Miller, "Man's 'unusual fixation' with Lebanese neighbors led to killing, Tulsa police say," *The Washington Post*, August 16, 2016,

https://www.washingtonpost.com/news/morning-mix/wp/2016/08/16
/mans-unusual-fixation-with-lebanese-neighbors-led-to-murder-tulsa-police
-say/?utm_term=.35a15258722e.

[16] Mark Berman and Samantha Schmidt, "He yelled 'Get out of my
country,' witnesses say, and then shot 2 men from India, killing one,"
The Washington Post, February 24, 2017, https://www.washingtonpost
.com/news/morning-mix/wp/2017/02/24/get-out-of-my-country-kansan
-reportedly-yelled-before-shooting-2-men-from-india-killing-one/?utm
_term=.0c58734e282c.

[17] "U.S. Muslims Concerned About Their Place in Society, but Continue to Believe in the American Dream," Pew Research Center, July 26,
2017, http://www.pewforum.org/2017/07/26/findings-from-pew-research
-centers-2017-survey-of-us-muslims/.

[18] Justin Parrott, "Jihād as Defense: Just-war theory in the Quran and
Sunnah," Yaqeen Institute, October 16, 2016, https://yaqeeninstitute.org
/justin-parrott/jihad-as-defense-just-war-theory-in-the-quran-and-sunnah/;
Qur'an 22:39-40.

[19] "Open Letter to Al-Baghdadi," http://www.lettertobaghdadi.com/.

[20] Erin Kearns, Allison Betus, and Anthony Lemieux, "Why Do Some
Terrorist Attacks Receive More Media Attention Than Others?," March 5,
2017, https://ssrn.com/abstract=2928138.

[21] Inés San Martín, "Pope Francis denies that Islam is violent," *Crux*,
July 31, 2016, https://cruxnow.com/world-youth-day-krakow/2016/07/31
/pope-francis-denies-islam-violent/.

[22] Jonathan A. C. Brown, *Muhammad: A Very Short Introduction* (New
York: Oxford University Press, 2011), 27.

[23] Carl Ernst, *Following Muhammad: Rethinking Islam in the Contemporary World* (Chapel Hill: University of North Carolina Press, 2004), 46.

[24] John T. McGreevy, *Catholicism and American Freedom: A History*
(New York: W.W. Norton, 2003).

[25] Richard Brent Turner, *Islam in the African-American Experience*, 2nd
ed. (Bloomington, IN: Indiana University Press, 2003).

[26] "U.S. Muslims Concerned About Their Place in Society, but Continue
to Believe in the American Dream," Pew Research Center, July 26, 2017,
http://www.pewforum.org/2017/07/26/demographic-portrait-of-muslim
-americans/.

[27] "Muslim Americans: No Signs of Growth in Alienation or Support
for Extremism," Pew Research Center, August 30, 2011, http://www.people
-press.org/2011/08/30/muslim-americans-no-signs-of-growth-in-alienation
-or-support-for-extremism/.

[28] "U.S. Muslims Concerned About Their Place in Society."

[29] Pontifical Council for Inter-religious Dialogue and the Congregation for the
Evangelization of Peoples, Dialogue and Proclamation, 1991, Vatican website,
http://www.vatican.va/roman_curia/pontifical_councils/interelg/documents
/rc_pc_interelg_doc_19051991_dialogue-and-proclamatio_en.html.

Chapter 3

[1] Thomas Ryan, "Interreligious Implications for Catholic Evangelization," in *Catholic Evangelization in an Ecumenical and Interreligious Society*, ed. Secretariat for Evangelization (Washington, DC: USCCB, 2004), 66.

[2] Francis Clooney, "'Nostra Aetate' Turns 50," *America*, October 27, 2015, http://www.americamagazine.org/content/all-things/churchs-irreversible-openness-nostra-aetate-50.

[3] John Kiser, *The Monks of Tibhirine* (New York: St. Martin's Press, 2002), 46, 148.

[4] *Testament of Dom Christian de Chergé* (1993); quoted in Christian Salenson, *Christian de Chergé: A Theology of Hope* (Collegeville, MN: Cistercian Publications, 2012), 200.

[5] de Chergé, *L'invincible espérance*, ed. Bruno Chenu (Paris: Bayard, 1996), 183; quoted in Salenson, *Christian de Chergé*, 58.

[6] de Chergé, unpublished correspondence, letter of June 7, 1981; quoted in Salenson, *Christian de Chergé*, 93.

[7] Francis, *Laudato Sì* (On Care for Our Common Home) 233, Vatican website, May 24, 2015, http://w2.vatican.va/content/francesco/en/encyclicals/documents/papa-francesco_20150524_enciclica-laudato-si.html.

[8] Kenneth Cragg, "The Tents of Kedar," in *Christian Lives Given to the Study of Islam*, ed. Christian W. Troll and C. T. R. Hewer, 7 (New York: Fordham University Press, 2012).

[9] C. Stenzel, "Alumni Spotlight: Amanda Stueve," interview with Amanda Stueve, April 11, 2015, http://kstateanthclub.com/?p=1095.

[10] Paul Moses, *The Saint and the Sultan: The Crusades, Islam and Francis of Assisi's Mission of Peace* (New York: Doubleday, 2009), 182.

[11] Ibid.

[12] Kathy Warren, *Daring to Cross the Threshold: Francis of Assisi Encounters Sultan Malek Al-Kamil* (Eugene, OR: Wipf and Stock, 2003), 83.

[13] Coleman Barks, trans., *The Essential Rumi* (New York: Quality Paperback Book Club, 1995), 51.

[14] James Fadiman and Robert Frager, ed., *Essential Sufism* (San Francisco: HarperOne, 1997), 87.

Chapter 4

[1] John Paul II, Address of His Holiness John Paul II to Young Muslims, August 19, 1985, Vatican website, http://w2.vatican.va/content/john-paul-ii/en/speeches/1985/august/documents/hf_jp-ii_spe_19850819_giovani-stadio-casablanca.html.

[2] Elahe Izadi, "Pope Francis washes the feet of Muslim migrants, says we are 'children of the same God,'" *Washington Post*, March 25, 2016, https://www.washingtonpost.com/news/worldviews/wp/2016/03/25/children-of-the-same-god-pope-francis-washes-the-feet-of-muslim-migrants/?utm_term=.a4c685983014.

[3] John Paul II, *Redemptoris Missio* (encyclical) 29, Vatican website, December 7, 1990, http://w2.vatican.va/content/john-paul-ii/en/encyclicals /documents/hf_jp-ii_enc_07121990_redemptoris-missio.html.

[4] Christian Salenson, *Christian de Chergé: A Theology of Hope* (Collegeville, MN: Cistercian Publications, 2012), 27–28.

[5] Jacques Dupuis, *Christianity and the Religions: From Confrontation to Dialogue*, trans. Phillip Berryman (Maryknoll, NY: Orbis Books, 2002), 225–26.

[6] Adnan Majid, "Rahmah—Not Just 'Mercy,'" MuslimMatters.org, December 3, 2012, http://muslimmatters.org/2012/12/03/rahmah-not -just-mercy/.

[7] William Chittick, "Divine and Human Love in Islam," in *Divine Love: Perspectives from the World's Religious Traditions*, ed. Jeff Levin and Stephen G. Post, 193 (West Conshohocken, PA: Templeton Press, 2010).

[8] Reza Shah-Kazemi, "God, 'The Loving,'" in *A Common Word: Muslims and Christians on Loving God and Neighbor*, ed. Miroslav Volf, Ghazi bin Muhammad, and Melissa Yarrington, 102 (Grand Rapids, MI: Eerdmans, 2010).

[9] John Paul II, *Crossing the Threshold of Hope* (New York: Alfred A. Knopf, 1995), 41, 92.

[10] James Fadiman and Robert Frager, eds., *Essential Sufism* (San Francisco: HarperOne, 1997), 199.

[11] Ibid., 204.

[12] Jamal Rahman, *The Fragrance of Faith: The Enlightened Heart of Islam* (London: Book Foundation, 2004), 70.

[13] Nevad Kahteran, "Fitra," in *The Qur'an: An Encyclopedia*, ed. Oliver Leaman, 210 (London, UK: Routledge, 2006).

[14] Davi Barker, "Fitra: Creation," *The Muslim Agorist*, Patheos, August 5, 2013, http://www.patheos.com/blogs/muslimagorist/2013/08/fitra-creation/.

[15] See this clip from the film *The Message*, directed by Moustapha Akkad, 1977, https://www.youtube.com/watch?v=LF2rFtZpA2Q.

Chapter 5

[1] John Paul II, *Redemptor Hominis* 6, Vatican website, March 4, 1979, http://w2.vatican.va/content/john-paul-ii/en/encyclicals/documents/hf_jp-ii_ enc_04031979_redemptor-hominis.html.

[2] John Paul II, *Recognize the Spiritual Bonds which Unite Us*, Thomas Michel and Michael Fitzgerald, 14 (Vatican City: Pontifical Council for Interreligious Dialogue, 1994); quoted in Douglas Pratt, *The Church and Other Faiths* (Bern, Switzerland: Peter Lang, 2010), 314.

[3] Christian de Chergé, "Prier en Église à l'écoute de l'Islam," *Chemins de dialogue* 27 (2006): 19; in Christian Salenson, *Christian de Chergé: A Theology of Hope* (Collegeville, MN: Cistercian Publications, 2012), 100–101.

[4] Ibid., 101.

[5] de Chergé, *Testament of Dom Christian de Chergé* (1993); quoted in Salenson, *Christian de Chergé*, 201.

[6] Daniel Madigan, "Nostra Aetate and the questions it chose to leave open," *Gregorianum* 87, no. 4 (2006): 785.

[7] Madigan, "A Lenten Journey," in *Christian Lives Given to the Study of Islam*, ed. Christian Troll and C. T. R. Hewer, 257 (New York: Fordham University Press, 2012).

[8] Christian de Chergé, *L'invincible espérance*, ed. Bruno Chenu (Paris: Bayard, 1996), 183; quoted in Salenson, *Christian de Chergé*, 58.

Chapter 6

[1] Vatican Secretariat for Non-Christians, The Attitude of the Church toward the Followers of Other Religions: Reflections and Orientations on Dialogue and Mission (Vatican City: Libreria Editrice Vaticana, Pentecost 1984), 30.

[2] Pontifical Council for Inter-religious Dialogue and the Congregation for the Evangelization of Peoples, Dialogue and Proclamation, 1991, Vatican website, http://www.vatican.va/roman_curia/pontifical_councils/interelg /documents/rc_pc_interelg_doc_19051991_dialogue-and-proclamatio_en .html.

[3] Claire Schaeffer-Duffy, "Lebanese interfaith group grounds work in 'spiritual solidarity' with the other," *National Catholic Reporter*, April 25, 2016, https://www.ncronline.org/preview/lebanese-interfaith-group -grounds-work-spiritual-solidarity-other.

[4] Ibid.

[5] Ibid.

[6] Ibid.

[7] Dorothy Buck, *Louis Massignon, A Pioneer of Interfaith Dialogue: The Badaliya Prayer Movement* (Clifton, NJ: Blue Dome Press, 2016).

[8] Christopher Bamford, "Badaliya: The Way of Mystic Substitution" (originally published online in *Second Spring—A Journal of Faith & Culture*), November 3, 2011, https://sophiacommunity.wordpress.com/2011/11/03 /sacred-hospitality/.

[9] Ibid.

[10] See video, March 14, 2013, https://www.youtube.com/watch?v=ycw DXhVRNZ0.

[11] Ibid.

Appendix C

[1] Exodus 34:6; Psalms 103:8; Qur'an 1:1.

[2] Qur'an 30:22; Qur'an 5:48.

[3] Qur'an 30:22; Qur'an 5:48.

[4] Qur'an 41:34.

[5] Mark 12:31.
[6] Leviticus 19:34.
[7] Qur'an 41:34.
[8] Qur'an 1:6.
[9] Qur'an 1:6.

Index